THE
MIDWINTER
MUSIC

A SCOTTISH ANTHOLOGY
FOR THE FESTIVE SEASON

THE
MIDWINTER
MUSIC

A SCOTTISH ANTHOLOGY
FOR THE FESTIVE SEASON

edited by Marjory Greig
assisted by Marjorie Wilson

with Illustrations by Joyce Greig
and Music transcribed by John Wood

SCOTTISH CULTURAL PRESS

First published in 1995 by
SCOTTISH CULTURAL PRESS
P O Box 106, Aberdeen AB9 8ZE
Tel: 01224 583777; Fax: 01224 575337

British Library Cataloguing in Publication Data
A catalogue record for this book
is available from the British Library.

ISBN 1 898218 21 8

Cover and internal layout design by Mark Blackadder.
Cover photograph by Walter Bell.
Typeset in 10/12 pt Times.
Printed and bound by Athenaeum Press Ltd, Gateshead, Tyne and Wear.

Ev'n then a wish (I mind its power)
A wish, that to my latest hour
    Shall strongly heave my breast;
That I for poor auld Scotland's sake
Some useful plan, or book could make,
    Or sing a sang at least.

~ Robert Burns ~

P R E F A C E

THE idea of assembling a collection from Scottish Literature and Music centred round the *Daft Days* – as the Festive Season used to be called – arose in me from a love of Christmas and a life-long attachment to the Mither Tongue. The final incentive erupted from reading in two anthologies published furth of Scotland, that our country paid scant attention to Christmas itself, concentrating solely on Hogmanay and New Year. There are areas of the country where this used to be true; but the assumption made me wonder what I had been doing these past seventy-odd Christmases, not to mention my parents before me! It led to four years of exploration in libraries and bookshops, searching out prose, poetry and ultimately music that portrayed and interpreted the multi-coloured facets of the Festive Season. The mine is rewardingly deep and rich in quantity and in quality.

Knowing that Marjorie Wilson shared my love of Christmas and attachment to all things Scottish, and having long admired her work, I asked if she would be willing to help me compile the book, and was delighted when she readily agreed. So we selected and arranged material that would quarter the country, span the centuries and provide something of interest to children and adults alike. This last point was essential – Christmas is for everyone; Scotland has made Hogmanay undeniably her own.

The project has now become a book. The necessity arose of finding someone to illustrate it. Joyce Greig, a Scottish-born Canadian artist, was only too happy to provide us with a set of delicate black and white illustrations and designs which beautifully complement the script. To round everything off, the music had to be transcribed, a task admirably and enthusiastically carried out by John Wood.

Our thanks go to the writers who have so willingly allowed us to use their works, to the publishers and owners of copyright for their interested co-operation, to Rena Richardson for her excellent typescript, to the staff of the Music Room in the National Library for their assistance in uncovering music that seemed to have been *made-to-measure,* to Mr R K Leslie and the staff of the Orkney Library for providing us so willingly with essential background information, and to friends and family who lent books and gave practical help. We are specially grateful to George Mackay Brown for allowing us to use *The Midwinter Music* as our title for the anthology.

One final note – in a country which supposedly has paid little attention to Christmas, the numbers of writers and musicians who have written about Christmas exceeds by far those who have written about Hogmanay!

Marjory Greig
Marjorie Wilson
EDINBURGH 1995

C O N T E N T S

Contents

Contents

Contents

Contents

PUBLISHER'S NOTE

THE extracts contained within this book are printed as originally written and/or published. Because of this, there may be a slight degree of conflict over spelling and consistency of language.

P R O L O G U E

NATIVITY

'Flist ower tae yon byre, loon,
Fin oot fut's the mineer;
The nowt beasts are waukrife
An' makkin a steer
An' yet in their lowein'
There's nae sign o' fear!'

'O Mither, come quick!
O Mither, come quick!
I got sic a begack
Ye'll nivver believe't!
There's yon lassie oot there
Wi' weird in her een
An' the chiel she caas Joseph –
Min' we saw them yestreen –
Gaun vaigin the causey
Disjaskit an' deen
Priggin' sair for a bield –
At the howff there was neen.

She's gotten a bairn
In the caul howdumdeid;
He's there in the strae
Whaur the nowt tak their feed –
A wee nyakit Knabbie
WI' A LICHT ROUN'S HEID!'

~ Lilianne Grant Rich ~

AWA IN A MANGER

Awa in a ruch heck, nae bield for a bed,
The bairnie Lord Jesus set doun his sweit head.
The starns in the dark lift sklentit doun whaur he lay –
A winkie-wee babby, asleep in the strae.

The kye, they are mooin, the babby's awauk,
But the wee thing, Lord Jesus, nae greetin he'll mak.
Bide near me Lord Jesus, leuk doun frae the sky
An stay in about me till mornin's ootby.

Bide near me, Lord Jesus, I ax ye tae stay
Cooried down close aside me an loe me, I pray.
Bless aa the dear littlins ye hird tenderly;
Mak us wordy o haiven tae dwall there wi Thee.

~ Music: *Traditional Gaelic Air;*
Words by *J Kirkpatrick;* owerset by *Marjory Greig* ~

SANTA CLAUS WAS NO BIG DEAL

WHEN we were children in Morar during the thirties and early forties, December invariably arrived accompanied by rain, strong winds and occasionally, snow and frost. The burns, ready to burst their banks, crashed and cascaded down the steep sides of the loch, and a thick mist often rolled down over the hills. On other days, however, we would awaken to brilliant sunshine and dazzling frost, when everything sparkled and footsteps rang out on the frozen ground.

With this ever-changing weather came the season of Advent, and a heady sense of anticipation made itself felt in the village, bringing to us children a feeling of happiness and terrific excitement. In school and in church we began to sing Christmas hymns and carols, while the Christmas story was unfolded to us week by week, as we were prepared in mind and spirit for the Christian Festival. At that time our Christmas was solely a Christian festival. There were no parties, nor any such frills and frivolities!

At home on our croft there were preparations of a different kind: the boat had been beached and safely tied up for the winter, the potatoes lifted and gathered into pits, and the peats, cut in summer from our peat bank beside Loch na Ghille Gobaidh, were ready to be brought in. Now at weekends, during the hours of daylight, we three girls, each bearing a small sack, would trudge up the hill behind Daddy, carrying one of full size, to bring back as many peats as we could shift, and after several forays, stack in the shed to dry out. Then there were the logs – with Daddy at one end of the cross-cut saw, and Mammy, our brother and the three of us all taking a turn on the other end, we sliced up the thick branches or sections of tree trunk into a fair show of logs. Hard work for a child, but we loved it!

In those days there were beautiful woods behind the croft, stretching across the hillside to Loch Morar. Our task during the weekend before Christmas, was a holly gathering expedition with Daddy. 'Never strip a tree,' he always said. 'Take what you need, and then go on to another. Then the tree will not be suffering.' We left some of the holly at the church, to be made into garlands; what we brought home was set along the kitchen mantelpiece and above the pictures. And that was the extent of our decorations. We never had a Christmas tree – there was no room in our small kitchen anyway; and with woods on our doorstep, any sunny, dew-bespangled morning, we could see a host of glittering fir trees – what need had we of a Christmas tree indòors?

Of far greater importance was the food. Mrs McVarish's tiny shop produced fruit for the cake, baked well in advance, and for the plum pudding that we all helped to make – weighing, pouring, stirring, wrapping up the trinkets saved from year to year, and the threepenny bits which always outnumbered the trinkets, stirring them all into the mixture as we wished our silent wishes, until the pudding was safely tied up at last and set on the range to boil in its big iron pot.

The range was fuelled by sticks, peat and a little coal, and everything was cooked on it. There was always a large iron kettle on the boil – a necessity as the house had no running water. We helped carry the drinking water from the well and the washing water from the burn at the bottom of our fields. While some of the houses in the village boasted running water, there was no electricity anywhere until the 'Hydro-electrics' came after the end of the Second World War; all our homes were lit by candles and oil lamps. Under Mammy's supervision we learned to fill the lamps and trim the wicks on weekdays, after school.

On Christmas Eve, preparations reached their climax: the hen, killed and plucked by Granny the previous day, was stuffed and made ready for the oven; we pared potatoes, chopped vegetables for the soup, prepared the Brussels Sprouts and carried out our other chores with special care.

At night, after the cows had been brought into the byre, fed and watered, and the one milking cow milked, we all washed hands and faces and dressed in our best. It was important to have something new to wear – a checked cap for Daddy, scarf for our brother, new knitted hats for us girls. (As we grew older, we learned to knit our own.) If one of us had a new coat, it was never worn until Christmas Eve, while Mammy always managed to get a new hat. This was the most important night of the year; we must not be found wanting.

At about 11.30 we set off for Midnight Mass, walking along the railway line as far as the station, before taking to the road, as the croft lay beyond the tracks. Every-body walked to church – the Bracara people from three miles up the lochside; Duncan MacDonnell ferried the Meoble people across the loch, before walking the final stretch from the jetty; others came from Camusdarach and Rhuachamhor, halfway on the road to Arisaig, joining the families en route who lived in Tougal, Kinigharry, Kinsadle and Rhubana, while many followed the railway line from Mallaig, including the Protestants who had no service in their own church.

If it was moonlight and a night of stars or frost, we children felt very excited. There was then no street lighting and night walks were normally dark and shadowy. But beautiful as the moonlight might be, it took the gradual appearance of the warm, flickering candle and lamplight in the church windows to bring home to us the full significance of the night. Not always silent nor still, it was undoubtedly holy.

The light of expectancy shining in our eyes, we went inside and looked to the rear of the church. Would the Crib really be there again? We were never disappointed. There before us stood a cave, about four feet in height, made out of stone simulated paper, with holly and evergreens round about it. A light shone down on the Baby Jesus, lying on real straw in the manger. Mary and Joseph, the shepherds and the Wise Men were there too, the ox, the ass and some sheep as well. The scene filled us with awe and immense happiness. This was Christmas, the spirit of Christmas – the

Child, born in a stable, come to save us all. Nor did the wonder of it diminish with the passing years.

At midnight the bell rang, Canon MacNeill began to celebrate Mass, and we knew that Christmas Morning had broken. With what fervour did we sing our hearts out in 'Lo, amid the Winter Snow', 'Silent Night', 'Away in a Manager' and 'Come, come to the Manger' – was it not here beside us, and we had come? Then Ishbel, a young girl with the voice of an angel, sang the 'Taladh Chriosta' or 'Christ Child's Lullaby', and that was the most beautiful of all –

> Mo ghaol, mo ghra'dh is m'eudal thu,
> M'iunntas ùr is m'eibhneas thu,
> Mo mhacan a'lainn ceutach, thu,
> Chan fhiu mi-fheinn bhith'd dhàil.

Mass over, all was stir and bustle outside as the adults shook hands, and, with cries of 'Nollaig Mhath!', wished one another a Happy Christmas, before heading home at the double, with no time now to marvel at the moonlight or the starry sky.

Mammy quickly poked up the fire before giving us all a hot drink with scones and shortbread. We hung up our stockings for Santa, confident that he would come and hoping that we might see him. Of course we never did, but the stockings were always there when we got up by candlelight, with an orange in the toe, an apple and some nuts. This was truly wonderful to us and we never looked for more: for there were no presents as we have today; only Mary Holden Bird, the artist who painted so many beautiful watercolours of the district, generously sent a present by post to every child in the village, year after year.

When the delights of our stockings had been savoured, everybody got on with the everyday chores – the milking cow to be milked, the others let out to pasture, eggs to be gathered, water and peats to be fetched. The range was cleaned out and kindled; the chicken was put into the oven, the pudding and vegetables set on the side to simmer. Then we all set off for Mass. Rain, hail, sleet or snow, our family went to church on Christmas Morning!

After church, the table was set, the soup was heated up and we all eagerly took our places round the table for the best, most delicious and certainly the most greatly enjoyed meal of the whole year.

This feeling of enjoyment saw us through the dish-washing and the clearing up, until Mammy stoked up the fire with more peats and the kitchen took on a warm, cosy and peaceful atmosphere. We played games all afternoon – Ludo, Snakes-and-Ladders, Snap – listened to records on the old gramophone, or even to the radio which normally was switched on only for the news or Scottish dance music, in order to conserve the batteries.

Before darkness fell, we dispersed to call the cattle home, feed and water them. The milking cow had to be milked again, and the last peats brought in for the night. By that time we were ready for a pot of tea, well brewed on the hob, hot-buttered scones, mince pies, Christmas cake and sometimes a black bun.

Of course we all ate more than usual; so Christmas night saw us pleasantly tired and ready for bed. Our two wonderful days had come to an end, but would be remembered far into the coming New Year. Santa Claus was no big deal for us: we never had visions of his arrival on a sleigh, loaded with toys. I believed in him until I was ten years old, knowing that the other children would get a stocking, and I was bound to have one too. We were so happy and contented in our simple lives, we never grumbled about not receiving presents. Indeed, we were unaware that children elsewhere had more, and the other children in the village were probably the same. Instead, Christmas was a family time of Christian faith. Morar has often been referred to as Blessèd Morar – our Festive Seasons were truly blessed. And as for all the never-ending, repetitive chores that had to be done, Christmas or no Christmas, we were all working the croft together, and they became a pleasure.

~ As told by *Mary MacDonald* ~

TALADH CHRIOSTA

~ Music: *Traditional Gaelic Air* ~

CASTLES IN THE AIR

The bonnie, bonnie bairnie, wha sits poking in the ase,
Glow'ring in the fire wi' his wee roond face;
Laughing at the fuffin lowe, what sees he there?
Ha! the young dreamer's biggin castles in the air.
His wee chubby face, and his touzie curly pow,
Are laughing and nodding to the dancing lowe;
He'll broon his rosy cheeks, and singe his sunny hair,
Glow'ring at the coals wi' their castles in the air.

~ James Ballantine ~

BACKGROUND

Frost, I mind, an' snaw,
An' a bairn comin' hame frae the schule
Greetin', nearly, wi' cauld,
But seein', for a' that,
The icicles i' the ditch,
The snaw-ploo's marbled tracks,
An' the print o' the rabbits' feet
At the hole i' the wire.

'Bairn ye're blue wi' cauld!'
An apron warmed at the fire.
An' frostit fingers rubbed
Till they dirl wi' pain.
Buttered toast an' tea,
The yellow licht o' the lamp,
An' the cat on the clootie rug
Afore the fire.

~ Helen B Cruickshank ~

WINTER

Noo that cauldrife Winter's here
    There's a pig in ilka bed,
Kindlin's scarce an' coals is dear;
Noo that cauldrife Winter's here
Doddy mittens we maun wear,
    Butter skites an' winna spread;
Noo that cauldrife Winter's here
    There's a pig in ilka bed.

~ Charles Murray ~

AN LATHA-FEILL MUIRE

AGUS anns an t-seathamh mìos, chuireadh an t-aingeal Gabriel o Dhia, gu caithir de Ghalile, d'am b'ainm Nasaret,

Dh'ionnsuidh òigh a bha fo cheangal pòsaidh aig fear d'am b'ainm Ioseph, de thigh Dhaibhidh; agus *b'e* ainm na h-òigh Muire.

Agus air dol a steach do'n aingeal d'a h-ionnsuidh, thubhairt e, Fàilte dhuit, o thusa d'an do nochdadh mòr dheadh-ghean, *tha* an Tighearn maille riut: *is* beannaichte thu am measg bhan.

Agus an uair a chunnaic i e, bha i fo thrioblaid inntinn air son a chainnte, agus a' reusonachadh ciod a' ghnè altachadh-beatha 'dh'fheudadh a bhi 'n so.

Agus thubhairt an t-aingeal rithe, Na bitheadh eagal ort, a Mhuire: oir fhuair thu deadhghean o Dhia.

Agus, feuch, gabhaidh tu a'd' bhroinn, agus beiridh tu mac, agus bheir thu Iosa mar ainm air.

Bithidh e mòr, agus goirear Mac an Ti a's ro àirde dheth; agus bheir an Tighearn Dia dha rìghchaithir 'athar féin Dhaibhidh.

Agus bithidh e 'n a Rìgh air tigh Iacoib gu bràth, agus cha bhi crìoch air a rìoghachd.

Agus thubhairt Muire ris an aingeal, Cionnus a bhitheas so, do bhrigh nach 'eil aithne agam-sa air duine?

Agus fhreagair an t-aingeal agus thubhairt e rithe, Thig an Spiorad naomh ort, agus cuiridh cumhachd an Ti a's àirde sgàil ort: uime sin an ni naomh sin a bheirear leat, goirear Mac Dhé dheth.

Agus, feuch, do bhan-charaid Elisabet, tha ise féin torrach air mac 'n a sean aois; agus is e so an seathamh mìos dhise d'an goirteadh bean neo-thorrach:

Agus thubhairt Muire, Feuch banoglach an Tighearna; bitheadh e dhomh-sa réir d'fhocail. Agus dh'fhalbh an t-aingeal uaipe.

~ Tiomnadh Nuadh (New Testament),
The National Bible Society of Scotland, 1935 ~

THE FORETELLIN O JESUS

IN the saxt month efter thae happenins, the Angel Gabriel wis sent frae God til a toun o Galilee caa'd Nazareth. He had a message for a lassie thair wha wis trystit tae a man caa'd Joseph, o the Hoose o Dauvid; an the lassie's name wis Mary.

The Angel said tae her, 'Joy be wi ye, favoured ane. The Lord is wi ye. Blissit be ye amang weemen.'

Mary wis frichtit at the say, an wunnert whitiver sort o message this micht be.

But the Angel said, 'Fear-na Mary, for ye hae gotten favour wi God. An tak tent tae me! Ye sall conceive an bring furth a son, an sall caa his name Jesus. He sall be michty, an sall be caa'd the Son o the Maist Hie; an the Lord sall gie tae him the throne o his faither Dauvid. He sall reign ower the Hoose o Jaucob for iver; an o his Kingdom thair sall be nae end.'

Mary said tae the Angel, 'Hoo sall this be, syne a guid-man hae I nane?'

The Angel quo, 'The Halie Speerit sall come an the poo'er o the Maist Hie sall come doon ower ye; an yer bairn sall be caa'd the Son o God. An mair! Elspeth, wha is kin tae yersel, is wi bairn in her auld age; she wha wis caa'd barren.'

'Lo, I am the servan o the Lord,' said Mary. 'May it be wi me accordin tae thy Wurd.' An the Angel gaed awa frae her.

~ Jamie Stuart ~

ISLAND ADVENT

I LOVE advent. There is something exciting about this time, when Christmas is coming closer .... Advent with its candles and lights, its secrets and symbols, is a special time, a month of small joys in the winter darkness.

It begins with the advent wreath, made of evergreen veronica twigs, fastened to a double circle of wire, and bound with scarlet ribbons. Four red candles are fixed into the circle, and lit one after another, until all four are lit on Christmas Eve. Candles are beautiful, warm and gentle, and their wavering flames light the kitchen every night. They are the best lights for Christmas, living and vibrant, stretching back into the past, bending and sputtering as doors open, and draughts swirl in from the cold night, flickering back to life, glowing yellow and clear again.

Advent is full of secrets, of presents hidden in cupboards under piles of sheets, when jerseys are waiting to be finished, and mittens and caps pile up in the wicker basket. There is never enough time, so time itself is a gift, when it is spent on making

something for Christmas .... There is no real Christmas shopping, so presents are difficult to buy and send.

It is a time for children, and for anticipation, for making cards and opening the doors and windows of the advent calendar, and for baking all sorts of things. William is good at making the Christmas cake, and he does the mixing, but everyone helps with fetching and measuring, cracking eggs, and stirring in the brandy. It is a communal effort, and all of us share the feeling of satisfaction at the lovely smell of the cake baking ....

We listen to carols on the radio, turning the dial to pick up programmes from Norway, Germany and France, as well. Carols are more evocative than anything else; they bring back the ghosts of lost Christmasses, when the words made indelible pictures on the mind, and their reality was unquestioned. Even now they make me shiver with the same magic, starry skies, shepherds and angels, and frosty winter nights.

If the steamer has reached the island, we have a real tree, the only one the children see, and its aromatic scent fills the room, reminding us of distant forests far away from this treeless island. Balloons soar away into the night sky from a child's hand. Cattle chew peacefully in the byre. Christmas is still a simple festival, a sharing of hearths, when everyone is together, the room is warm, and the advent star fixed on to the light shines out through the window, golden into the dark.

~ Christine Muir ~

THE BIRTH O JESUS

A N it cam tae pass in thae days, thair gaed oot a decree frae Caesar Augustus that aa the inhabiters o his dominions suld be registrate. This wis tae be made whan Cyrenius wis Governor o Syria; an aa war gaun tae be registrate, ilk ane til his ain toun.

Joseph as weel gaed up frae Galilee, oot o the toun o Nazareth, intil Judea, intil Dauvid's toun whilk is caa'd Bethlehem; for that he wis o the Hoose an stock o Dauvid. He gaed tae be registrate wi Mary, his betrothed wife, wha wis a mither-tae-be.

An so it wis that while they war thair, the day cam for her tae gie birth. An she brocht furth a son, her firsten-born, an she rowit him in swaddlin claes an beddit him in a manger, for that thair wisna room for them i' the inn.

THE ANGELS' SANG

N oo thair war, in the same launs, shepherds bidin in the fields an keepin gaird ower thair flocks by nicht. An see! an Angel o the Lord cam til them, an the glorie o the Lord glintit roon aboot them.

They war sair feart, but the Angel said tae them, 'Be-na frichtit, for I bring ye guid tidins o muckle joy tae the hale warld. For thair is born tae ye this day in Dauvid's toun, a Saviour wha is the anointit Lord. An here is the sign for ye – ye sall find the bairn, rowit in swaddlin claes, liggin in a manger.'

An aa at aince thair wis wi the Angel a thrang o Hevin's host, praisin God an sayin, 'Glorie tae God in the heicht o Hevin, an on the erthe, peace, guid-will towards men!'

Whan the angels gaed awa frae them towards Hevin, the shepherds said ane tae anither, 'Lat us gang noo intil Bethlehem an see this thing that has come aboot, that the Lord has made kent tae us.'

An they gaed, makin haste, an fund Mary an Joseph thair wi the bairn, wha wis liggin in a manger. An whan the shepherds saw him, they gaed awa an telt abroad the wurds that war telt tae them anent this bairn.

Aa wha heard had grete wunner at the things telt tae them by the shepherds, but Mary keepit aa thae things, ponderin apon them in her hert. An the shepherds gaed back til thair fields, giein glorie tae God for aa they had seen an heard, e'en as it wis telt them.

THE BAIRN IS NAMED

A N on the aucht day, whan the bairn wis tae be named, they caa'd him Jesus, whilk wis the name the Angel had telt Mary tae gie him.

~ Jamie Stuart ~

MARY'S SANG

~ Music by *Maureen McDougal* ~

MARY'S SANG

Wisht ma wee bairnie, o hushie baloo
Wisht ma wee mannie, o coorie doon noo!
Ye're snod in the strae wi' yer mammie sae near
Awa fae the stishie o' Bethlehem's steer.

CHORUS: Wisht ma wee bairnie, o hushie baloo!
           Wisht ma wee mannie, o coorie doon noo.

There's een that's the Laird o' earth and o' sea
Fa's gien ye, ma laddie, tae Joseph an' me;
Bit, gled though we are, in oor herts we baith ken
He'll need ye some day tae tak back for His ain.

CHORUS:

Last nicht, fin the star blinkit bricht up abeen,
Cam hameower shepherd laddies, wi' stars in their een,
Tae tell o' the glory they'd seen as they cam,
Wi' a lamb for a present tae Mary's wee lamb.

CHORUS:

And syne, booin doon afore Joseph an' me,
Three skirie-like lads fae awa ower the sea
Three wee gowden boxies for playocks they bring
Wi' fey words in their mous as they spak o' a king.

CHORUS:

I'm wae fin I think o' hoo lanesome I'll be
Fin you're king in the kingdom, sae far abeen me
But aye there's ma hope that ae day ye will gie
The same joy tae the world that ye noo bring tae me.

CHORUS:

~ Words by *Joyce Collie* ~

CHRISTMAS CAROL

'Twas a cauld, cauld nicht i' the back o' the year;
The snaw lay deep, and the starns shone clear;
And Mary kent that her time was near,
As she cam to Bethlehem.
When Joseph saw the toon sae thrang,
Quo' he: 'I houp I be na wrang,
But I'm thinkin we'll find a place ere lang;'
But there wasna nae room for them.

She quo', quo' she: 'O Joseph loon,
Rale tired am I, and wad fain lie doon.
Is there no a bed in the hail o the toon?
For farrer I canna gae.'
At the ale-hoose door she keekit ben,
But there was sic a steer o' fremmyt men,
She thocht till hirsel': 'I dinna ken
What me and my man can dae.'

And syne she spak: 'We'll hae to lie
I' the byre this nicht amang the kye
And the cattle beas', for a body maun try
To thole what needs maun be.'
And there amang the strae and the corn,
While the owsen mooed, her bairnie was born.
O wasna that a maist joyous morn
For sinners like you and me?

For the bairn that was born that nicht i' the stra'
Cam doon frae Heaven to tak awa'
Oor fecklessness, and bring us a'
Safe hame in the hender-en.
Lord, at this Yule-tide send us licht;
Hae mercy on us and herd us richt.
For the sake o that bairnie born that nicht,
O, mak us better men!

~ Alexander Gray ~

NAE ROOM

Nae room, Mistress, the inn is fu',
Nae shelter here for him an' you;
But there's a cave whaur oxen gang –
He wad be warm them amang.

Aye, Mary, come awa in-by,
Here i' the troch he'll cosy lie.
Eh, but he's bonny! Safe frae harm
The stirkies' breath will keep him warm.

The shepherds cam, the Wise Men tae,
An' by the bairnie knelt tae pray.
(Hoo can ye sae contentit lie
There i' the manger wi' the kye?)

A cot o' gowd wad be mair meet,
Wi' angels gaithered roon' his feet –
A palace, Mary, no a cave
For him wha cam tae seek an' save!

'Na, ye are wrang,' I hear her say,
'Love couldna win oor he'rts that way.'

~ Jamie A Smith ~

NAE BRANKIE BAIRN

Nae brankie bairn this,
We're no' weel-aff ava;
His gift frae me wis but a kiss,
A troch his beddie-ba.

The swirlin' snaw smoors a',
But warm the beasties' breath …
Dad will mak ye a cradle braw
Whan hame in Nazareth.

I'll mind whit angels telt,
An' whause ye really are;
I'll ne'er forget the joy I felt,
The brichtly-shinin' star.

But Oh! I lang for spring
An' us baith hame wi' you,
Whan in my airms I'll rock my king,
Liltin a lillilu.

~ Jamie A Smith ~

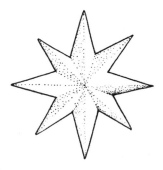

THE DOG AND THE MANGER

THE old collie dog was tired as he lay beside his master on the hillside that lovely moonlit night. His master was a shepherd who watched the sheep all night through to take care of them, because in these days long long ago there were many wolves and foxes. The shepherd had two young dogs he'd reared up and kept along with the old collie, but he loved and respected his old collie most because he'd had it for many many years. So they sat on the hillside and the moon rose higher; it was beautiful and the stars were shining.

The shepherd turned round and said to the collie, 'Old fellow, you must be tired. You ran a lot this morning, more than you should have, and you know you're getting old now. I'm sure there's no use the four of us sitting here. Why don't you go home and go in the byre, sleep among the hay for the night? It'll make you fresh for tomorrow. Me and your young offspring here will take care of the sheep.'

The old collie dog sat up, his tongue hanging out, and he looked at his master. He wondered why his master didn't want him. He understood the language all right, but some things his master said he didn't really understand. When the master said 'go home old friend', he knew the meaning perfectly. He thought to himself, 'My master doesn't need me this night so I'll go home.' He really was tired.

So the old dog trotted back to the small steadings and the farm where he lived. He curled up in the byre among the hay and straw that had been placed in the stalls. And his old friend the donkey came in from the cold; he was a free agent who wandered around the farm to his heart's content. And the collie couldn't remember when he'd ever seen the place without the donkey. The donkey walked into one of the stalls and started chewing on the hay or straw or whatever was left out. The collie curled up to go to sleep. He heard his friend the donkey chewing, chewing, chewing on and on and on.

Then a little later he heard voices coming through the doorway. He wondered, 'Is that my master coming home?' And he looked out. It was still dark but the moon was shining clear. He thought to himself, 'It can't be my master, it's not his time yet. He always comes home by daylight when the sheep'll be safe.'

So he was wide awake and sitting in the stall one down from the donkey, when, lo and behold, who should walk to the stall beside him but a woman! A young beautiful woman and a man with a beard. The collie had never seen these people before and he wondered who they were. He said to himself, 'They must be strangers seeking their lodgings for the night.'

So the dog curled back, he never said a yelp, never said a bark. He watched them; the man took his wife by the hand and led her into the empty stall that had little straw in it. And there was a manger above them for holding the hay for feeding the cattle, but there were no cattle in the byre this night. The dog sat and he listened, he heard the man talking and he knew well what they were saying.

The man said, 'This is where we'll stay; we shall find shelter here for the night.' He looked around, 'It's only a dog and a donkey and I'm sure they won't disturb us .... Are you all right my dear?'

'Well,' she says, 'I don't feel very well.'

And the man rakes up the hay, places it, makes a little bed. He says, 'I'm sure ... will it happen tonight?'

She says, 'I think it'll happen in moments.'

The collie dog, he's sitting there. The donkey stops chewing his hay and all is quiet.

And then, lo and behold, the man says, 'Are you needing any help?'

'No,' she says, 'I'll manage myself. Just you stand there at the stall entrance and see that I have a little privacy for a few moments.'

And the man stands there ... he walks back and forward. And the dog lies, he never says a word, but he hears everything that is going on .... The next thing the dog hears is the crying of a little Baby ... a little Baby cried.

And the dog said, 'This woman, this being, this human being must be giving birth to a baby right here beside us in the stall. I have never seen this before.' And he crawled slowly round a wee bit closer, he keeked round the stall. Lo and behold the woman was holding up the most beautiful little Baby that you ever saw. It had long dark golden hair. It was still wet.

And the husband ran in. He pulled off his covering of cloth, his cloak. He told her, 'Use this!' And his wife wrapped the Baby in it.

She said, 'He's a wonderful child.'

Then the husband said, 'We need some place to put him for a wee while.'

And she said, 'Put some straw in the manger just above where I lie, and put him there for a few moments.'

The husband shook the straw along the manger and he took this little baby wrapped in his own cloth, he stood naked to the waist, and he put him up in the manger. And the old collie dog ... he saw the most beautiful thing he ever saw in his life: he saw a star shining through the window. The star seemed to come closer and closer and closer – till it shone right above the window. The dog had never seen this before and he wondered why such a star had come so close .... his thoughts were on his master in the hillside. He wondered if his master would be disturbed by this same shining star. But then his thoughts changed; he heard the man and the woman talking.

He said, 'Look, we must stay here for the night. But we must find better shelter for our child tomorrow. I'm sure he will be all right, though; nothing's going to happen to him. He's a lovely child.'

The old dog sat and listened to all they said. And the Child never said one word.

Finally the talking stopped and the dog fell asleep. But he wakened early in the morning when he heard a disturbance next to the stall where he lay. This was the man and his wife getting up and taking the Child from the manger where he lay during the night.

And the man says, 'I must go to the village to find some help for you. There must be someone there who'll give you help.'

She says, 'I feel well, husband; I feel fine, lovely.'

He says, 'I know you feel lovely, but I must find some help for you and the Child.'

She says, 'Husband, it's a long way to the village. We passed it through and they wouldn't give us any shelter and that's why we ended up here.'

He says, 'We'll go back with the Baby, and when they see the Baby they'll probably give us shelter.'

'But,' she says, 'husband, I'm too weak, I can't walk.'

'Oh,' he says, 'don't worry, my dear, don't worry. You'll no need to walk. There's a little donkey here and I'm sure the farmer won't mind if I borrow it for a few hours to take you to the village.'

So the man walked in and took a rope, a halter from the wall. He put it on the donkey's head, but no saddle or bridle or anything. He lifted his wife up and placed her on the donkey's back. He went to the manger and picked out the wee Child, put him in her arms.

And the old collies's sitting watching this. He wonders and he wonders, wonders .... If his master knew about this .... what a story he could tell if only he could speak to him!

Then daylight came and the man with the beard, with not a stitch on his body because his cloak was wrapped around the Baby, walked out the doorway, leading the donkey with the woman and the Child. And he walked away.

The collie had never seen anything like this before in his life. He wondered, 'Would he ever see his old friend the donkey again?' But he loved that little Child and he wished he had seen him closer. He crawled up in the straw and fell asleep.

The next thing he heard was a whistle – his master was back from the hills with the two young dogs. He came before them with a large tray of food and put the dogs in the byre. Then the shepherd walked to his little cottage beside the farmhouse to have his own breakfast. But the old dog didn't feel like eating .... He just wanted one thing in his life that he'd never had – to look at the Baby because he had never seen His face.

After the young dogs had fed themselves, they curled up and went to sleep, and the old collie dog went to sleep too.

How long he slept he doesn't know, but the next thing he hears is 'hoof hoof' beats on the floor. In comes the old donkey, just by himself. And instead of going to his own stall, he walks into the stall where the old dog lay.

The old collie looks up, says, 'Hello, old friend, you're back.'

And the donkey speaks to the dog, 'Yes, I'm back. I had such a wonderful experience. I walked to the village and I carried this beautiful young woman and her child. But,' he added, 'I feel queer and funny now.'

'And did you see the Baby?' says the collie dog.

'Yes,' says the donkey, 'I saw the Baby, the most beautiful Baby in this world.'

And the old collie says, 'I wish I had seen the Baby.'

'You will,' says the donkey, 'some day you will see Him. He will come again. He will come again and everyone will understand. But not talking about Him or talking about you ... ,' says the donkey, 'do you see something strange about me?'

'No,' says the collie, 'I don't see anything strange about you. You're just a donkey to me and I'm just a dog to you.'

'Look again,' says the donkey. 'Look once more. See if there's something about me that you've never seen before.'

And the collie looks and says, 'You've four legs like me and you've got a tail; you've got a head and ears like what I've got. You've got a mane and hair – just like me.'

'No,' says the donkey, 'there's something else you must see and I hope in the future many people will see it, for when they see it, they'll probably understand!'

'Understand what?' says the collie dog. 'Tell me what you mean!'

'Look on my shoulders,' says the donkey, 'and tell me what you see.'

The collie stood up, he put his front paws up against the wall and he looked. The donkey wasn't very high. He looked on the donkey's back, and, lo and behold – for the first time in his life – across the donkey's shoulders was *the cross* in black. 'What's that?' said the collie who had never seen this before.

'That,' said the donkey, 'is the mark of the Child who was born this night. It was given to me and will remain with me for eternity, until some day He comes and shows his face to everyone.'

'Then maybe I'll see Him,' said the dog, 'maybe I *will* see Him again?'

'You'll see Him,' said the donkey, 'you'll see Him again; maybe *not in this world, but maybe in another one* when we leave this place.'

And that is the end of my story.

~ *Duncan Williamson* ~

CAROL SERVICE

IT wis a snell day an darkenin faan we got tae the Savoch kirk an we sat on the hard pews an sang aboot Royal David's city an the lowin cattle an the baby waukenin but nivver greetin.

Ootside, in the frost, the howes fulled up wie the haar o the caul nicht comin but we waur far awa, in some ither December place, faar fortaivert herds chittered wie dreid faan the glory shone, an syne they grippit their staves an made for Bethlehem an the bairn in a spare troch. In the bleak mid-winter he wis born, an far fae hame, an beddit faur the kye waur. We sang aboot the 'snow had fallen, snow on snow' an we could see't for wirsels as clear as day, snaa driftin an faain an happin the roch edges an the shairp lines, makkin a saft blur o posts an palins an the bare trees o wids lang leafless.

~ David Ogston ~

CHILD IN THE MANGER

IT was Mairi Macdonald on the Island of Mull who gave Scotland her favourite carol, 'Child in the Manger', which is sung at Watch Night services throughout the land. Mairi was the wife of a crofter, Lachlan McInnes, and was born in Mull in 1789. She never learned to read or write, but she used to croon her little songs to the island children, and at ceilidhs among her friends and neighbours who passed them on. She composed the words to the Gaelic air of the carol at the height of a religious revival which swept the Inner Hebrides during the 1820s.

Mairi died in 1872; two generations later, in 1959, a cairn was erected in her memory near her birthplace at Ardtun, and all who use the Iona ferry may see it. Her Christmas hymn lives on.

Malcolm Macfarlane of Elderslie got the original Gaelic air from an old man, a native of Mull, and made a translation of the words. It was not until the twentieth century that a later translation was made by Lachlan MacBean, a Gaelic-speaking native of Kiltarlty, who was a journalist in Fife and died in 1931. It is his words, in general use today, that will always mean Christmas to Scots children.

~ Introduction by Amy Stewart Fraser ~

CHILD IN THE MANGER

Child in the manger,
   Infant of Mary;
Outcast and stranger,
   Lord of all!
Child who inherits
   All our transgressions,
All our demerits
   On him fall.

Once the most holy
   Child of salvation
Gently and lowly
   Lived below;
Now, as our glorious
   Mighty Redeemer,
See him victorious
   O'er each foe.

Prophets foretold him,
   Infant of wonder;
Angels behold him
   On his throne;
Worthy our Saviour
   Of all their praises;
Happy for ever
   Are his own.

~ Music: Traditional Gaelic Air;
Words by Mairi MacDonald; translated by Lachlan MacBean ~

NATIVITY PLAY

To cheer us in the Winter
    bright Christmas Roses grow,
And we have scarlet holly
    and pearl-white mistletoe.

Fruits of misguided science
    are comfortless to me,
And there is little solace
    in cold theology.

No matter – we are able
    to rise again and go
To see the starlit stable
    among the Winter snow:

To see the light above it
    and enter by the door,
As men for generations
    have entered there before;

The Magi in their wisdom,
    the shepherds from the hill,
The donkey and the oxen –
    the door is open still.

The Baby that was given
    and cradled in a stall,
He brought from highest Heaven
    the light of hope to all.

~ Vagaland ~

THE BAIRNIE JESUS – A CAROL

Bairnie laich amang your strae,
born to be oor Prince this day,
noo you lie in manger bare,
stots and kye aa thrangin there.
And yonder in the cauldrif nicht
the star o Bethlehem lowes bricht.

But syne into the bothy's stir
wi gowd and frankincense and myrrh
the Magi come and thankful kneel,
taen by the star to wish you weel.
And 'herds forbye, aa croodit roon,
fleggit by angels, noo bow down

and worship in the steir and stour
the Love that's born on earth this hour.
The Word is gaen the shape o man –
a bairnie's livin oot God's plan –
and sae at Christmastime we sing
ower aa the warl 'Jesus is King!'

~ Ken Morrice ~

CHRISTMAS BELLS

Whin you waakened up, a peerie sheeld,
   Ida hert o a Winter nicht,
An you heard da soond o da muckle wind
As he shook da hoose in a moorie-blinnd,
   You langed fir da moarnin-licht.

Whin dey wirna a blink fae da restin-paets,
   No a emmer sheenin red,
You wir blyde ta hear da hens ida byre
An you wissed at da dug wid laeve da fire
   An set him aside your bed.

Dan cam da nicht whin Minnie said
   At Santie Klaas wid come,
Wi his lang red cott an his graet big shön
An his face da sam as da red hairst-mön
   As he oagit doon da lum.

You never tocht about wadder dan,
   If hit wis rain or snaa.
Fir you kyent at nedder wind or weet
Or hailie-shooers or sweein sleet
   Wid budder him ava.

What tochts comes in a bairn's mind,
   Whin he's shaltered safe at haem!
Bit toil an care shön comes ta aa
An da laand o youth is far awa
   Laek a half-forgotten draem.

Bit hit aa comes back at Christmas-time
   Whin we sit at wir ain hert-sten
We hear da bells o da reindeer-slaidge
An we tink o da Star an da lang, lang vaige
   At wis med be da Tree Wise Men.

~ Vagaland ~

THER CAM A SHIP

Ther cam a ship fair sailland then,
Sanct Michael was the steires-man,
Sanct John sat in the horn.
Our Lord harpit, our Lady sang
And all the bells of heav'n they rang
On Christonday at morn,
On Christonday at morn.

~ Traditional ~

25

THE MIDWINTER MUSIC – CHRISTMAS

IN the northern islands December is a dark month. The lamps are burning when people go to their work. Light thickens again in the early afternoon. The weather, more often than not, is cold and stormy. There are also calm clear nights when the hemisphere of sky is hung with stars and in the north the Aurora Borealis rustles like curtains of heavy yellow silk.

It is the season of The Nativity. It is also the time of trows.

To the islanders the earth they tilled was an element of dark dangerous contending energies. The good energy of the earth raised their crops into the sun and rain and wind; but there were other earth energies bent on famine, sickness, death. These energies were active always; especially in the dark cold time of the year when nothing grew, the earth seemed to belong to them entirely. The island farmers knew this evil brood as trows, and the trows were more than vague abstract energies, they had shape and substance; they could dance, they could speak, they could travel between the hill and the ploughed field, they were often seen (but only by people who had the gift). The trows belonged to the under-world, to the kingdom of night. Hideous shapes, they represented all the curses of unredeemed nature. The best way to contain the kingdom of winter and death was to lead a decent life, for the trows were among other things embodiments of the seven deadly sins; and it was best to observe duly the rituals of Christianity as well as other rituals that were old when the mega-lithic people built the stones at Brodgar.

The corn and the animals had to be protected. The trows grew strong and bold in winter in proportion as the creatures of light paled and dwindled. Straws in the form of a cross were fixed to the lintels of barn and byre. So these places were 'sained', made holy. The most precious creatures in a croft, and the most liable to corruption, were the children. A special care was taken of them on Helya's Night, the twentieth of December. In Shetland, the old grandmother went round each bed and cradle and committed the young ones to the care of the Virgin Mary.

> Mary Midder, had de haund
> Ower aboot for sleeping-baund,
> Had da lass and had da wife,
> Had da bairn a' its life.
> Mary Midder, had de haund
> Roond da infants o' oor laund.

This beautiful poem was being uttered in the north three and a half centuries after the Reformation.

If the children were not protected it was easy for the trows to steal them. What happened was this: the trows left their own offspring in the cradle, and these winter children generally grew up sick and deformed. So the people say of someone who looks permanently ill that he is 'trowie'.

A great peace and silence fell on the islands on Thomasmas, the twenty-first of December, and continued till after Christmas. No work was done, except what was absolutely essential.

> The very babe unborn
> Cries O dul! dul!
> For the breaking o'
> Thammasmas Night
> Five nights afore Yule.

They called December the twenty-third Modra Night. It was the longest night of the year and so the mother of all other nights. And possibly it was the night when the Mother of God, heavy with her burden, set out on the road to Bethlehem.

December the twenty-fourth was a night specially holy and terrible. The trows, in dark hordes, lingered outside every croft. The crofter removed the upper quern-stone from the lower. All through the year the women had ground the corn, turning the quernstones in fruitful sunwise circles. It was certain that the trows, given the chance, would secretly turn the quern widdershins, against the sun, so that the stones would be rendered barren and the family would starve during the following year.

The terror of darkness was held in check by a strictly-observed ritual. The mother brought out a basin and filled it with water. The man of the house, priest-like, took three live embers from the fire and dropped them in the water. So, in midwinter, the elements of fire and water were true to the tryst of purification ....

In this condensed drama all nature – light and darkness, the four elements, plant and beast and man – were seen as part of a divine festival. The creatures of nature kept their trysts in season, they could not behave otherwise. Man, with his scattered and distracted energies, the flesh tugging forever against the spirit ... moving between the trow-infested earth and the angel-fretted sky, proclaimed his allegiance to the kingdom of light (of which he was the shining wayward heir) in the form of a willed and strictly-observed ritual; as now, when the priest-like crofter, his dwindled fields all around him, mingled the elements of fire and water; for a purification, that his winter-beleaguered household might be worthy to eat bread, a mingling of his own harrow-sweat with heaven's grace .... One by one, each member of the family washed himself all over in the fire-kissed water and put on clean clothes. The rooms had been swept already; everything dirty had been bundled away; the dishes on the dresser glinted in the lamplight. The children were put to bed. Midnight was approaching. The other members of the family retired one by one, until only the parents were left. They made then an act of great faith. Though the night outside was thick with trows, they unfastened the door and left the lamp burning and went to bed. It was possible that Our Lady and Saint Joseph with their as-yet-hidden treasure would come to their croft that night, seeking shelter.

Early on Christmas morning the man of the house rose before daybreak, while the others were still asleep. He lit a candle in the skull of a cow, carefully fixing it in the eye-socket. He went into the byre, carrying this lantern. He fed the beasts by its light, giving them more to eat than usual. It was a re-enaction of the scene in the byre at Bethlehem; the animals had also been present at Christ's nativity. The flame in the skull was a reminder to them that they shared both in mortality and in this blessed time, the kindling of the one true light in the world's darkness.

There was nothing to be afraid of now. The trows had returned to their burrows, defeated. Christ was born among the fields.

The children were awake when the crofter came back. They had a small candle each that they lit and set here and there about the room. The crofter filled a bowl with whisky – quintessence of earth's ripeness, the heavy rich blood of summer; solemnly he carried the bowl to each person in turn; even the children had to wet their lips. The bread lay on the table – not the coarse everyday bannock, but Yule-brunnies, little round yellow cakes of rye and fat, pinched at the edges to represent the sun's rays; a Yule-brunnie for everyone in the house. The Christmas breakfast was a festival of candle light. The eating of the cakes was a kind of pre-Christian non-sacramental communion. In the heart of winter they devoured the sun, and so filled their days with light and gaiety and fruitfulness.

~ George Mackay Brown ~

DA TROW'S CHRISTMAS

As I looked ower da briggy stanes,
I caught a glimpse o da trows.
I ran doon da path on tae da knowe,
An dere I saw dem.
Dey said tae dir peerie boy, Tirval,
'Noo come doo an geng tae dy bed.'
'Bit, mam, I want tae hing up me sock,
I want tae wait fir Santi tae come.'
'Noo, Tirval, geng tae dy bed noo or
I'll skelp dy tail!'

So Tirval geed tae bed hinging up his sock.
'Night, night Tirval,' I quietly said,
'I hope Santi comes an laves dee a lok.'
An wi a run an a giggle,
I geed hame tae bed,
An took da advice Tirval's mam had said!
Happy Christmas Tirval Trow!

~ Claire Henry, aged 11 ~

TATTIES FROM CHUCKIE-STANES

ONCE upon a time there was a poor lady that lived beside the forest. She had an awful lot of children, an sometimes it was pretty hard fir her because she didna have a husband. She scraped and scratched as much as she could, she used tae take in washin an sewin an things fir tae keep the children alive – she had aboot seven or eight o' them, all wee steps an stairs, ye know!

An it cam roon about Christmas time. She had nothing tae give them, not a thing in the house, but she had nae idea whar tae get anything. They start't askin fir something tae eat. So tae keep them quiet she start't tellin them stories, but the stories wisnae fillin their stomachs. They said, 'Mammy, we want somethin tae eat, boil us some potates!'

So tae brighten their hearts up a wee bit, she goes out tae the front o' the house. There used tae be a wee brook runnin past the house many years ago, an durin the summer when times wis better wi her she'd gathered all the bonnie wee white stanes, we call 'em 'chuckie-stanes', an pit them round her garden path. So she took her pot an filled it full o' stanes, put water on 'em, shaken some salt on 'em an put them on the fire. It was one o' thon old-fashion't fires wi the big old-fashion't arm that comes oot the side – she hung the pot on.

All her kids gather't round. 'What are ye doin, Mammy?' says the little one.

She says, 'Youse asked fir potates an I'm going tae boil ye some. A hope youse enjoy them because they'll take a long while tae boil' – thinkin in her own mind, 'be the time thae "potates" wis supposed tae be boiled the hunger would leave them and they would all faa asleep.'

But she didnae know ... who had restit on the windaesole but a woodland fairy! It had landit an heard what wis goin on. An the fairy felt very sad – the mother wi all the children should have nothing but everybody else in the village had plenty – specially comin nearer Christmas. So the fairy cast a spell on the pot.

The pot begun tae boil and the children wis saying, 'Mammy, lift the pot off now, lift the pot off an see – the potates is boiled!' Mammy liftit it off, poured the water off; it was only stones she had put in the pot. All the wee children gather't round. But when she lifted the lid off there wis the most beautiful potates ye ever saw in yir life, dry as anything, jist burstin up like flowers!

An the lady was surprised – she felt that God .... 'At least,' she says, 'A've got potates – but hoo in the world?' She says tae hersel, 'It must ha' been a fairy.' So she liftit all the potates oot an pit them on a nice plate on the table. She gave them all round tae all the bairns, and there were nothing left fir hersel. So she looked in the bottom o' the pot. All the wee scrapins o' tatties that wis left – she took a spoon an says tae hersel, 'This'll have tae be enough fir me.' She scraped the bottom an put them on a plate, but when she turned up the spoon it was full o' gold sovereigns! An she scraped the pot clean till she had a full plate o' gold sovereigns. She stood an scratched her head, 'A wonder,' she says, 'whar that could come fae? Because they werenae in the pot when A put them stones in fir the bairns tae boil. Some lucky fairy must ha' been thinkin o' me the night when she done that fir me.'

So she washed all the potates off the gold sovereigns, took the money an told the oldest one, 'You look after the wee ones ti' A come back, an A'll no be long.' She run doon tae the village, intae the shops an she bought everything she could think of: decorations fir the house, yon big Christmas bells, oranges an apples, all the fruit, nuts an everything, presents fir every one o' them, ti' she wis loaded an couldnae carry no more. An she still had gold sovereigns left cause the fairy had gien her plenty. She gev her children the best Christmas they ever had in their life; they were happy blowin on things an puttin paper hats on their heads. They didnae know it wis a wee woodland fairy that had given them that lovely Christmas, and that's the last o' ma wee story.

~ *Duncan Williamson* ~

DECEMBER DUSK IN THE SOUTH SIDE

IT was dark by four in midwinter, and coming home from school in the December dusk to tea in the dining room with the fire blazing and the red silk shade of the low-hanging chandelier lit up by the bulbs inside, one was conscious of a theatrical shift in scene, as of a curtain lifted.

And in the streets outside, the little fruitshops and fancy goods stores and grocers, decorated for the Christmas season, with mounds of tangerines set in half globes of silver paper, with net stockings filled with cheap toys and bells of coloured paper hanging in the window, would repeat the theme in a different key: festive windows lit in the darkness to challenge the December murk. On a clear day the dusk would turn true violet in colour, and the dark outline of the Castle would stand out on the horizon in romantic gloom. (Many years later they took to floodlighting it, which was picturesque but not the same thing: the gas light in the windows of the little shops in the back streets, with their tinsel decorations and cheap Christmas goods, was the most moving illumination I ever saw in Edinburgh.)

We did not observe Christmas, of course; we kept instead the more or less contemporary Jewish festival of *Chanukah*; but the Christmas atmosphere always seemed proper and acceptable, and it never seemed to me that I was in any way cut off from it in virtue of our not keeping the actual day. And the coloured *Chanukah* candles, and my father's tenor voice leading us in the old hymn of *maoz tsur*, 'Rock of Ages', mingled in my mind with the illuminated windows, with the silver tangerines and the box of crackers and the loops of tinsel, with the old Castle looming black in the purple evening and the sense of the darkening city beyond falling away to the Firth of Forth. *Chanukah* was Edinburgh in December.

It was strange, I suppose – thought it did not seem strange to me then – this easy blending of Christmas and *Chanukah*, of Jewish history and Edinburgh atmosphere. *Chanukah*, the Feast of Lights, commemorates a miracle wrought in the Temple after the successful revolt by Judas Maccabeus and his heroic companions against the paganising forces of Antiochus Epiphanes .... Yet *Chanukah* to us was also the distribution of 'pokes' of sweets to Jewish children after the special service in the Graham Street synagogue, and walking home afterwards in the dark December evening, savouring the atmosphere of Edinburgh at night during the Christmas season.

There was, of course, much less commercial ballyhoo about Christmas then than there is now, and besides, Scotland, whose established Presbyterian Church had long minimised celebration of Christmas Day as 'Popish', celebrated the season rather than the day.

The real Scottish festival was Hogmanay, New Year's Eve, in which we could participate as a purely secular feast. Jewish New Year was a solemn occasion, the ushering in of the period of penitence which culminated in the Day of Atonement ten days later; the Scottish New Year was an utterly different sort of affair, and though we never celebrated it as a family, we were at liberty to identify ourselves with its celebration by others.

I am not sure if I have set out all the factors in their proper logical emphasis. Perhaps there were other reasons for what, in retrospect, I can see as the effortless reconciliation of a very Jewish *Chanukah* feeling with a very Edinburgh feeling of celebration. I doubt if I would even have considered this worth commenting on if I had not been struck with the way in which Jewish parents get fussed about the Christmas problem today. It is a problem that I never remember once being bothered about in my childhood. (But no sooner have I written this than I ask myself whether it is wholly and absolutely true. I seem to remember a faint twinge – of regret? of simple envy? – when the red mail vans came up our street, delivering Christmas presents, and I knew they would not stop at our door.

~ David Daiches ~

THE CHRISTMAS TREE 1976

An American aviator
 fleein owre auld Selkirk toon
Saw an awfee queerlike sicht
 as he was lookin doon.
It was something as peculiar
 as he had ever seen –
Fourteen wee blobs o black
 roond a bigger blob o green.

He landed then at Turnhoose
 his thochts were troubled sair
He cam on doon tae Selkirk
 tae enquire a wee bit mair.
He asked an aged Souter
 at the tap end o the Green
Tae explain the ancient ritual
 that he had thocht he'd seen.

The auld man thocht a bittie
 while champin wi' his jaws
An said, 'If they were movin,
 then Ah'm shair they wad be craws.
Bit if they werenae, then
 Ah think oo'd aa agree
It was fourteen cooncil workmen,
 Pitten up oor Christmas tree.'

~ Walter Elliot ~

THE CHRISTMAS TREE MARCH

~ Music by *Angus Cameron* ~

CANDLE CULPRITS

THE staff are suddenly decimated. No fewer than six teachers are absent and as word comes trickling through about them, it appears they all have 'flu.

For the next few days we all have giant-sized classes – doubling-up they call it. This has the effect of not merely reducing the education by half, but reducing it to zero. There are 'doubles' every day until the teachers begin to trickle back, one by one.

The matter is complicated by the approach of Christmas.

No one knows just what the full import of Christmas means unless she has been in a school at that time. To hang decorations in any classroom in this school would require an extending ladder like the Fire Brigade's. As the invalids slowly come back all looking very peely-wally, we begin to make paper chains to festoon the walls with.

A Christmas tree is hailed with delight, but setting it up is a kind of engineering problem. The class has gone on a foray to the public park, which rises to steep woody heights behind the school. They bring back stones to supply ballast for the box in which we are to put the tree. Other heavy objects are commissioned to help out the ballast, notable among these being short lengths of lead piping. The donors of these are Willie McIntosh and Geordie Ferguson.

'Where did you get these, Willie?' I ask.

'My father gi'ed me it.'

'Where did he get it?'

'In the yaird.'

'The shipyard?'

'Aye.'

'I thought he had no job just now?'

'He's back,' says Willie.

It could be true. There is the sound of an occasional hammer during the last few days. A small dredger is under construction in one of the yards ....

So we put the sections of lead piping into the box. I think it is unlikely a police raid would find it there! With the addition of plasticene and the stones, we manage to keep the tree upright. I buy some candles and we put them on the tree, but they are not to be lit until the last afternoon before the holidays. By the time I have stayed after the bell at four o'clock and added some tinsel, it is nearly dark. The tree stands all alone in the empty classroom as I close the door and go down the uncannily quiet stair. There is nothing in the world more lonely and empty than a school when all the children have gone.

I hasten away into the December dark.

*   *   *

It is Monday morning and the children are all round my desk before I reach the classroom. They surge forward, breathless and excited, the Clipe in the vanguard.

'Please, miss, somebody's stealt the caunels.'

'Stolen – not "stealt",' I say.

I examine the tree. Every candle has gone. Everybody looks suspiciously at everybody else.

'Maybe it was Jeanie,' says the Clipe.

Everybody looks at Jeanie McSweeney. (Adam McSweeney in Primary 7 is sometimes suspected of picking up golf balls up at the Golf Course, so the origin of the deduction is clear.)

'Herbert. That is not so. I was the last to leave on Friday.'

Everybody looks suspiciously at me.

'I shall have to think about this,' I say. 'Off you all go to your seats.'

I ask the janitor, who scowls as if wrongfully accused. No, he admits reluctantly, there has been no break-in at the weekend.

Throughout the day, the Clipe suggests some wild solutions to the mystery, until I am forced to forbid any more excursions out to my desk.

I have only two classes today instead of three, but we still have to say a lot of poetry. I try to vary the too-popular nursery rhymes instilled in the Infant Department …. Primary 3 insist on repeating all the rhymes they have learned on the ground floor. Willie McIntosh volunteers to come out and say his piece, but alone and unsupported in front of the class, he bashfully stumbles through the only rhyme so far not repeated a dozen times:

> 'He ran – up – the candle-stick –
> The little mousie brown –
> To – eh – eh – steal – and eat – eh – tallow –
> and – eh – '

I catch sight of the Clipe on his feet wildly waving his hand in the air.

'I know, Herbert – you're going to say it must have been the mice after all.' And it is. Now that we seem for the moment to have got rid of the rats, the mice have moved in. We put a few more candles on the tree before we leave, and next morning there are obvious traces of mice below the tree. The cleaners don't appear to have noticed anything to sweep up.

I keep the remaining candles in a tin box in the cupboard until the last day of term. I buy rosebuds, Smarties and Dolly Mixtures from Miss Purdie's wee sweetie-shop in the Sugar Alley, and spend the evening wrapping them into paper crackers.

* * *

The last day has finally arrived. There is a festive air about the school, warmed up further by the prospect of salary. The interval is longer today, and somebody brings sultana cake and shortbread for our tea.

The children all get their sweetie crackers, and we put the new candles on the tree and light them, watching carefully to see that all is kept safe. A gasp goes round the darkening room. After that there is no sound but crunching.

~ Janetta Bowie ~

OFF FOR THE HOLIDAYS

IT was nearing the Christmas holidays, and a great deal of talk now went on as to what they were going to do, where they were going to spend the time, and so on. One interesting occupation was the making of the paper bags to hold the cake and bun which each boy received when he left for home. A number of copy books were secured and the leaves sewn into large square bags into which the good things were to be put when breaking-up day came; that time being carefully calculated, not only by days, but by hours and minutes.

On the afternoon before Christmas Day they followed in line into the store, where each received a small, round, seed cake covered on the top with red sugar and having the letters 'G. H. H.' in white, as well as a square cake of shortbread and two oranges.

On the large deal table was a pile of 'doses', for which no one had any concern at present, whether they were 'auld or new baken, fan or plain'. It seemed as if the big-handled knife with which Shinnie cut the 'doses' in two was going to have its holidays as well. The large bin for the meal, and the beer barrel on its stout gauntrees were quietly ignored, although, at any other time the contents of the latter would very probably have been tested if the chances had been in favour of the knaps.

Old Clyde, Shinnie's dog, sat blinking at each boy as he received his lot, as much as to say, 'Take care of bun fever, my boy'. When the recipients arrived outside, the bun and cake were bagged in the paper pock, and were rolled up in the black bag which contained their change of clothing *etc.*

Walter and his chums made their way out, clear of the 'Wark' until the second day of January.

~ Jamieson Baillie ~

CHRISTMAS AT THE MANSE OF CRATHIE

WHAT pictures form when I conjure up the Christmas of my early childhood! A magic blend of bright fires, winking baubles, the feel of a rustling stocking in the dark and the excitement when its bulges were explored at daybreak!

No matter how severe the weather, Christmas at home was always merry!

Preparations began in good time. Cards were bought and posted early. Our parents had cards selected from a catalogue; we children had a fine selection of two-penny packets of six cards, complete with envelopes, from the general merchant in Ballater, and they were by no means of poor quality. We sent and received a great many cards. Postage was a ha'penny per card. We helped to wrap Christmas parcels using brown paper and string; decorative wrappings had not then come our way.

Armfuls of greenery were brought in; sprays of larch, ivy, and holly were placed behind every picture. Mistletoe we never saw, but we garlanded every room with paper-chains and an occasional Japanese lantern. Had we thought of a Yule log it would undoubtedly have been of sweet-smelling birch, but birch-logs were no Yuletide novelty. My father cut a fresh tree from the plantation every Christmas. Sometimes it was a little fir, sometimes a young Norway spruce, the tree which is said to have grown in Scotland before the Ice Age. We trimmed it with fragile glass ornaments similar to those available today. Handled with extreme care, and packed after use in cotton-wool, they lasted for years; they became a little shabbier each year but shone with all the magic of the season and were part of our traditional Christmas, as were the spiral candles in holders of painted tin in the shape of squirrels and birds, which clamped firmly to the tree.

On Christmas Eve we hung up our stockings on the brass knobs of the big double bed which Ellie and I shared. While still very young we had learned the verses by Clement Clarke Moore, which begin,

> Twas the night before Christmas
> When all through the house
> Not a creature was stirring,
> Not even a mouse.

We looked for Santa's arrival in his miniature sleigh with eight midget reindeer, and knew all their names ... Dasher, Dancer, Prancer and Vixen; Comet, Cupid, Donner and Blitzen.

We lay awake as long as possible, hoping to hear small noises that would indicate that our stockings were being filled by Santa, but invariably fell asleep till the blissful dawning of Christmas morning. Then came the first fumbling in the dark and the triumphant announcement to sleepy parents, 'He HAS come! He HAS come!' The contents of our stockings lacked novelty, but always gave us pleasure. Every year there was an apple, an orange, a watch on a chain (you could wind it and move the hands), a handkerchief, a little red jumping-jack or a monkey on a stick, crayons and a painting-book, and a new penny in the toe.

Handkerchiefs were printed with a coloured border and a fairy-tale picture. The picture practically disappeared at the first washing, but we had a new hankie for every special occasion. They were bought in the general merchant's shop for tuppence.

A bought stocking of red and white net stitched with scarlet wool, hung alongside our own. It, also, had familiar contents: a variety of doll's house toys, such as scales, grater and rolling-pin, tiny pasteboard dominoes or playing cards, inch-square picture-books, life-like tortoises in glass boxes which moved head and legs when gently shaken, and sticky pink sweets in the toe. Christmas dinner comprised a chicken with savoury stuffing, and a dumpling rich in fruit and candied peel, followed by figs, dates, almonds, and juicy raisins.

The feather-weight plastic fruit of today is the modern counterpart of the wax fruit which was the pride of many a Victorian hostess. My mother produced for the Christmas side-board a bowl containing an apple, pear, peach and tangerine. Each had a leaf attached, and a ring by which it could have been hung on the tree.

We had great fun with inexpensive crackers made of coloured transparent paper called gelatine paper, fringed at the ends and decorated with a scrap. Inside were musical toys such as miniature bagpipes, bird-warblers, and harmonicas; others contained the usual mottoes, paper hats, trinkets, and ugly grey snakes which uncurled in the creepiest way at the touch of a lighted match.

There were also parlour fireworks at half-a-crown a box. Each cracker promised a comical head-dress and an amusing novelty such as 'electric light, Japanese scintillettes, fire balloons, and shooting pictures'.

In later years many merry Christmas days were spent at Crathie Manse when the Rev. S. J. Ramsay-Sibbald was parish minister and Chaplain to the King .... He and his wife were close friends of my parents. They were the soul of hospitality and there was generally a large house-party for the festive season.

We went to church on Christmas morning for a carol service, and after lunch watched the trimming of the tree in the cosily-carpeted hall, and the placing of the angel on its highest point.

It was tall and glittering, wonderful beyond words, illuminated by candles which burned throughout the afternoon. The angel was rewound from time to time so that she continued to revolve slowly, the musical box inside her giving forth Christmas music. She wore white tulle shot with silver, and a star in her hair. In one hand she held a scintillating wand, in the other a trumpet close to her lips. She had yellow hair, and blue eyes forever staring into space. The mingled scent of spruce and candle-wax was part of the atmosphere. After tea, we assembled for the dismantling of the tree, a ritual in which the maids were always included. How they managed to spare time from the preparation of Christmas dinner I cannot tell, but as soon as they had

received their presents they disappeared again. They wore, at that time of day, black dresses, starched aprons trimmed with Swiss embroidery, and fly-away caps. Caps with streamers had gone out of fashion and muslin aprons were not yet in vogue. When a maid woke us in the morning she wore a sprigged print dress, a plain cap, and a starched apron with a wide bib, and went crackling from room to room carrying brass cans of hot water, pulling up blinds and wishing us a bright 'Good morning'. In those days, maids provided their own uniform so when each heard her name called at the stripping of the tree, she was delighted to step forward to receive the conventional gift of a length of pretty print or of good black 'stuff' for a new dress.

Ellie and I were all a-quiver when our turn came to receive a mystery parcel, wrapped in white tissue paper and gaily-beribboned.

Welcome gifts from our parents at this season, as on birthdays, were books, but at Crathie Manse all sorts of charming trifles came our way, and how we cherished the bonny bangles and beads! Once I received a miniature replica of the white feather fan favoured by Lily Langtry.

The Christmas dinner table at Crathie Manse was a splendid sight, with gleaming goblets and silver, crackers in profusion, and bon-bon dishes filled with sweets, chocolates and crystallized fruits. No crackers were pulled till the remains of the turkey, plum pudding and mince-pies had been removed and a toast drunk to the King. The crackers were a delight to the eye. They were known as cosaques, fashioned in richly-coloured paper and decorated with favours like a wedding-cake. All the children in the party, wearing paper hats, made a point of returning to the dining-room when it was deserted. The grown-ups were relaxing in the study, a cosy room preferable to the drawing-room on winter evenings, the maids were enjoying their own Christmas dinner, the table not yet cleared. Acquisitive little scavengers, we retrieved trinkets left lying among the nut-shells, novelties discarded by unthinking adults, gelatine paper which made stained-glass windows for dolls' houses, and flower-sprays from the cosaques.

Next day, after lunch, we Glen folk set off for home, walking over the Stranyarroch ....

~ Amy Stewart Fraser ~

A CHRISTMAS PRAYER

I'm jist a humble tractorman, I kenna foo to pray
But I aften fa to thinkin – plooin here oot on the brae –
Wi' the gulls aa flockin roon me like sae mony marble doos –
I've been coontin ower my blessings: they're fyles mair than I can use.

I look up to the lift abeen and ken Ye're near me Lord
An maybe ye'll forgie me if I try to say a word.
It winna be the wye they pray in kirks aa ower the laan
But somehow in yer wisdom, Lord, I ken Ye'll understaan.

It's comin on to Christmas, I hae beef and neeps and brose,
But there's them that winna hae sae much: tak peety Lord on those.
Let nae livin thing be hungry, lat nae livin thing be cauld,
Be it bird or beast or bairn or the helpless or the auld.

Gie saft warm beds to them that's ill or near their journey's eyn,
I aften think aboot tham as I lie sae snug in mine.
Let nae drunken dad or mither thrash or kick or bruise their bairn;
Spread Yer heavenly wings aboot them; dinna lat them come to hairm.

The fyou bit words I'm sayin Ye could hardly ca a prayer.
I jist ask as good as I hae got for mankind everywhere
So that aa oot ower the warld when the stars are glintin bricht
There'll be Peace and Joy and Plenty on this blessed Christmas nicht.

~ Lilianne Grant Rich ~

MACDUFF CHRISTMAS CAKE

1 lb currants	1 tablespoon treacle
1 lb sultanas	10 oz plain flour
4 oz glacé cherries	1 teaspoon mixed spice
4 oz mixed peel	½ teaspoon ground cinnamon
8 oz ground almonds	½ teaspoon ground ginger
8 oz butter; 5 eggs	¼ teaspoon ground cloves
8 oz soft brown sugar	¼ teaspoon ground mace
3 dessertspoons sherry	¼ teaspoon ground nutmeg

Cream the butter and sugar. Add the eggs whole, one at a time, and beat in the treacle. Add the flour sieved with the spices, then the dried fruits, cherries, peel and ground almonds; lastly pour in the sherry. Cook in a preheated oven (350°F, Gas 4) for 30 minutes, then turn down the heat to 325°F, Gas 3 and bake for about another 2½ hours. Line cake tin with double greaseproof paper.

~ Ena Baxter ~

TO MAKE SHORT BREAD

Take a Peck of Flour, put three lib of Butter in among a little Water, and let it melt, pour it in amongst your Flour, put in a Mutchkin of good Barm; when it is wrought divide it in three parts.

Roll out your Cakes longer than broad, and gather it on the Sides with your Finger. Cut it through the Middle, and job it on the Top, then send it to the Oven.

~ Mrs McLintock ~

MINCE PIES

FILLING:

1½ lb stoned raisins	3 tablespoons marmalade
1½ lb currants	5 apples; 5 lemons – juice and rind
1½ lb suet	3 lb brown sugar
4 oz candied peel	1½ teaspoons brandy

Peel and chop the apples, grate the lemon rinds. Mix all together and moisten with the brandy. This is an old family recipe from Craigievar, Aberdeen, 1893, which is very juicy and keeps well.

~ Mrs T S Drew ~

CHRISTMAS

How soon it starts,
The endless moan:
'Just ten more weeks,
How time has flown!
The shopping's such
An awful bore;
Things cost so much –
(And more, and more) –
I wonder if this colour suits her
 – Let's give the children a computer!'
Unchanging times remain, it's true:
The card that means
'I think of you'.
Is there a hopeful little sock
Hung by the fire, beneath the clock:
Name stuck on with a safety-pin,
For Santa's bounty to go in;
An apple and an orange too,
A coin pushed down into the toe,
And loving parcels set below
For Christmas morn?
The perfect way to celebrate
That long ago a child was born.

~ Jay ~

SANTA

My Grannie minds when Santa Claus
Cam ridin on a sled.
His reindeer ran along the ruifs
When bairns had gane to bed.

In Mither's day the aeroplane
Begoud to be the craze
And Santa yaised the new machine
Except on snawy days.

For Santa's aye been modern
And means to keep his place.
This year he's on a rocket comin
Stourin in frae Space.

~ J K Annand ~

SUNTY

Loon in his beddie.
Hearin' lika soon,
Speerin at his faither,
Een growen roun' –
Far did he come fae?
Fut dis he dee?
Foo can his reindeer
Flee owre the sea?
Fa maks the toys, Dad?
Foo dis he ken

Fut Jeannie asket
Tho' awa fae hame?
The lum's lang an' narra,
Fire's affa het,
Wid he nae be better
Comin' throwe the yett?
Sunty Maun be magic
Tae win doon a lum
Think ye Aa'll be lucky, Dad
An' get a muckle drum?

~ Music: *traditional;* arranged by *Adam Hamilton;*
Words by *James D Glennie* ~

NEW CHRISTMAS

~ Music by *John Anderson* ~

LETTER TO MY GRANDCHILDREN

AT first we South Yell folk kept the old style Christmas and New Year. That was
Christmas on 6th January and New Year on the 13th – it had something to do with
calendars being altered all over the country, but it took a long time to get into every
village. In the Auld Haa we had five socks to hang up, and Santa never missed us –
he always put an orange or an apple down in the toe, and then sweets and small
toys to fill up. In the early twenties I think it would be, other districts began to
change over and keep Christmas on 25th December like they do now. I mind the
Cuppaster folk speaking it over and all agreed to change it at the same time. Santa
got the message somehow, and there was no problem. For a year or two afterwards
we used to hang up our socks, new style in December, and also old style in January.
Good old Santa, he got to know about that too and always turned up!

~ *D G Sutherland* ~

THE THIRD SANTA

JENNIFER stood under the Christmas tree in Needles and Anchors' Depart-
mental Stores. A queue of chattering boys and girls stretched in front of her
waiting to go into a little house to see Santa Claus. She shifted impatiently from
one foot to the other. The more she thought about it, the more peculiar it all seemed.
She had already visited two toy bazaars and in each one there had been a Santa
Claus. And here was yet a third Santa in Needles and Anchors. Jennifer was puzzled.

As she waited, the long pointed icicles hanging from the roof of the little house
turned from silver to crimson in the bright lights of the store, then gradually back from
crimson to silver again. Jennifer stood there, trying to make up her mind what to ask
the third Santa for. She wanted, far more than the doll's house she had asked from the
first Santa; more than the doll with rooted hair she had asked from the second Santa;
and more, much more than she wanted the doll's pram, the baking set or the pots and
pans she had asked for in her letter to the Santa who lived somewhere far away in the
Black Forest; something she wanted more than anything else in the world. And that
was the desk.

The desk had a top that rolled up and disappeared somewhere down the back
leaving a flat bit to write on. It had three big drawers at one side and a space to tuck
your feet into underneath. The trouble had been knowing which Santa would be the
most likely to give it to her. The first Santa had had very fine red boots. But then the
second Santa's beard had been much longer and thicker and he had sat on a throne.
Still, for some reason, Jennifer had put off just a little longer asking for the desk.
Suddenly, she heard a voice calling 'Next please', and found she was at the head of
the queue at last.

The third Santa was sitting in a big chair before the fire. His feet, in a pair of very
old red carpet slippers, were thrust out towards the warmth. He swept some holly
paper from a chair and beckoned Jennifer forwards. She noticed as she sat down
that only a few miserable pieces of white fur clung to the edges of his robe and the
third Santa was hurriedly stitching some cotton wool on to the bare patches.

'Had to send my fur to the workshop,' he explained. 'Never been such a demand
for white rabbits. Every second child wanting to give white rabbits. Are you
wanting to give white rabbits?' A pair of piercing blue eyes darted a quick look at her.

Jennifer didn't reply. She sat with her mouth slightly open watching Santa's
needle pop in and out of the cotton wool like a small silver dagger.

'Jennifer, eh?'

Jennifer sat bolt upright. She had not said a single word, yet here was the third
Santa calling her by name.

'A pretty name – Jennifer. I expect they call you Jenny at home?'

Jennifer nodded. The third Santa bit through the thread and stuck the needle into a red velvet pincushion. He settled himself comfortably in his chair, placed the tops of his fingers together and wriggled his toes. 'And what are you giving for Christmas?' Jennifer frowned. For a moment she thought Santa had said *giving*.

'I'm wanting a desk, please, a desk with a top that rolls backwards, a flat bit to write on – three drawers at one side – and – a space to tuck your feet into underneath.'

'That's what you're wanting, is it? A desk with a top that rolls backwards and a flat bit to write on?' Santa sat back in his chair so that his face was no longer rosy in the firelight. Suddenly he sounded very tired. 'You didn't hear what I said, I think. I asked what you were giving at Christmas.'

'Giving?' Jennifer repeated the word as though it was the first time she had ever heard of it. 'Oh, I don't think I'm giving anything.'

The third Santa looked at her sadly. 'Not giving? At Christmas time? Everybody gives something surely.'

Jennifer wriggled in her seat. 'Well, actually, I do give something. I give away some toys.'

Santa sighed with relief. 'Of course you do. A little girl called "Jennifer" would give something. And it's not easy to give away shiny new toys we'd like to keep for ourselves.'

'Oh, it's not new toys I give away, just the ones I'm tired of. Last year it was Teddy because he had lost an eye and – and – Annabelle because her nose was broken.'

'I see. And no white rabbits at all?'

Jennifer shook her head.

The shabby red slipper Santa had been dangling from one foot fell to the floor. His big toe was sticking through a very large hole in his sock, and to hide it he hastily thrust his foot into the slipper again. Then he sighed and drew a book from his pocket. Written on the cover were the words 'Santa's Giving and Getting Book'. The book fell open at a page marked 'Jennifer' and opposite her name were two columns. In the right hand column which was headed 'Getting', Santa wrote 'writing desk'. Under the column marked 'Giving' he wrote the word 'NOTHING' in large capital letters.

Jennifer stood at the door watching the icicles turn from silver to crimson then back from crimson to silver in the bright lights of the store. 'I didn't ask any of the others for the desk,' she said.

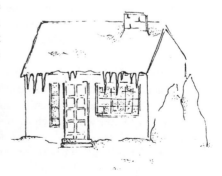

The third Santa smiled down at her. 'And that's a good sign. A very good sign indeed.' Then just as he was shutting the door of the little house, he bent down and whispered, 'Jennifer, I didn't use my indelible pencil.'

Jennifer was half way home when she came to the Pet Shop – and through the Pet Shop window she found herself staring straight into the pink eyes of a white rabbit.

A man came to the door rubbing his hands. 'The last white rabbit in the shop. Seems everyone's giving white rabbits this Christmas.'

Jennifer went in and lifted the rabbit from his hutch. He was silken and silver-white.

'You won't find another rabbit like him in this whole town. Tell you what, seeing he's the last, I'll let you have him for 50 pence. There's a bargain for you – what d'you say?'

'Will you keep him for me, please, till I come back? I've spent all my money at the Bazaars.' And in no time at all Jennifer had run home and was back at the Pet Shop with 50 pence jingling in the pocket of her tunic. When she reached the Pet Shop for the second time, the window was empty and the white rabbit was nowhere to be seen. Inside the shop, a boy was standing. Jennifer saw the white rabbit cradled in his coat.

'I hear you've bought him,' the boy said.

'Do you want him? Did you ask for him for Christmas?'

'I want him all right, but I didn't ask for him. I didn't ask for anything. You see, my Mother's ill in hospital. I expect Santa will forget all about me this Christmas.' He thrust the rabbit into Jennifer's arms.

'Your name's "David", isn't it? And don't you live in the next house but one to us?'

The boy nodded. 'That's right. We only moved in last week. And now Mother's taken ill and we're pretty unhappy.'

When Jennifer got home her Mother looked up from her ironing. 'Jennifer, why didn't you tell me you wanted a rabbit? Santa Claus might have brought you one if you'd asked.'

'It's not for myself. It's to give to somebody.' Jennifer carried the rabbit out into the garden and put him in the hutch where she had once kept hamsters. Later she mixed together some oatmeal and tea leaves for the rabbit's supper. 'Mother, what happened to the socks I was making at school last year – you remember – the red ones?'

Her mother sighed. 'Yes, I remember dear. You never finished the second one. All those mistakes and dropped stitches. Oh, Jennifer!'

'Do you think if I tried very hard I could finish them in time for Christmas?'

'I really don't know why you chose red, darling. Daddy can't possibly wear red socks at the office.'

'They're not for Daddy. They're for somebody who needs them terribly, terribly badly. I must finish them, Mummy.'

Carefully her Mother folded up the last piece of ironing and hung it over the clothes-horse to air. 'I see, then I'm sure you'll find the socks if you look in my work basket and, after tea, I'll help you to pick up all those dreadful stitches. If they're to give as a present they must be properly finished off, Jenny.'

All that week Jennifer sat and knitted. Round and round the needles with the bright red wool she knitted stocking stitch, row after row. Sometimes she dropped a stitch and sat with her mouth pursed up until she managed somehow to weave it into position again. At last, on Christmas Eve, with a little help from Mother, she reached the intakes at the toe and the socks were finished. That same evening, just before darkness fell, Jennifer and her father carried the hutch with the white rabbit secretly into David's garden. She knew that David was at the hospital visiting his Mother. Then the last thing Jennifer did before jumping into bed was to wrap the red socks carefully in shiny red paper and tie the parcel with silver string. She wrote 'Santa' on a tiny label and laid the parcel beside her stocking.

A robin singing at the window wakened her early on Christmas morning.

The desk was standing at the foot of her bed – the desk with a top that rolled backwards, a flat bit to write on, three drawers at one side and a space to tuck your feet into underneath. Jennifer lifted the top and there on the flat bit lay the page from Santa's 'Giving and Getting Book'. In the column marked 'Giving', Santa had rubbed out the word 'NOTHING' and written in 'One pair red socks and one white rabbit. Well done, Jennifer!'

~ Marjorie Wilson ~

ROBIN REIDBREIST

Robin, Robin Reidbreist,
Happin on a brier
Oot amang the snaw and ice,
While I sit by the fire.
Tell me in your bonnie sang
That ye're my frien sae true,
And I sall gie ye meat and drink
The hail winter throu.

~ *J K Annand* ~

COCK ROBIN'S COURTSHIP

Cock Robin rose up early
At the skreich o day
An gaed tae Jenny's windae
Tae sing a hush-a-bae.
He sang Cock Robin's love
Tae the wee bit Jenny Wren
An whan he cam on tae the end
Then he begoud again.

~ *Traditional;* owerset by *Marjory Greig* ~

JENNIE WREN

Jennie Wren, ye sing sae crouse,
And yet ye're neither blate nor a mous,
Creepin into hidey-holes
Whan huntin roond the elm boles.

Jennie Wren, I like your nest,
It's biggit snodder nor the rest,
Wi ruif and door, and lined wi hair
To bield ye frae the caller air.

Tell me, Jennie, is it true
That Robin Reidbreist cam to woo,
and whan he speired ye for his wife
Ye chased him for his very life?

~ *J K Annand* ~

THE MARRIAGE OF
ROBIN REDBREAST AND THE WREN

THERE was an auld gray Poussie Baudrons, and she gaed awa' down by a water-side, and there she saw a wee Robin Redbreast happin' on a brier; and Poussie Baudrons says: 'Where's tu gaun, wee Robin?' And wee Robin says: 'I'm gaun awa' to the king to sing him a sang this guid Yule morning.' And Poussie Baudrons says: 'Come here, wee Robin, and I'll let you see a bonny white ring round my neck.' But wee Robin says: 'Na, na! gray Poussie Baudrons; na, na! Ye worry't the wee mousie; but ye'se no worry me.' So wee Robin flew awa' till he came to a fail fauld-dike, and there he saw a gray greedy gled sitting. And gray greedy gled says: 'Where's tu gaun, wee Robin?' And wee Robin says: 'I'm gaun awa' to the king to sing him a sang this guid Yule morning.' And gray greedy gled says: 'Come here, wee Robin, and I'll let ye see a bonny feather in my wing.' But wee Robin says: 'Na, na! gray greedy gled; na, na! Ye pookit a' the wee lintie; but ye'se no pook me.' So wee Robin flew awa' till he came to the cleuch o a craig, and there he saw slee Tod Lowrie sitting. And slee Tod Lowrie says: 'Where's tu gaun, wee Robin?' And wee Robin says: 'I'm gaun awa' to the king to sing him a sang this guid Yule morning.' And slee Tod Lowrie says: 'Come here, wee Robin, and I'll let ye see a bonny spot on the tap o' my tail.' But wee Robin says: 'Na, na! slee Tod Lowrie; na, na! Ye worry't the wee lammie; but ye'se no worry me.' So wee Robin flew awa' till he came to a bonny burn-side, and there he saw a wee callant sitting. And the wee callant says: 'Where's tu gaun, wee Robin?' And wee Robin says: 'I'm gaun awa' to the king to sing him a sang this guid Yule morning.' And the wee callant says: 'Come here, wee Robin, and I'll gie ye a wheen grand moolins out o' my pooch.' But wee Robin says: 'Na, na! wee callant; na, na! Ye speldert the gowdspink; but ye'se no spelder me.' So wee Robin flew awa' till he came to the king, and there he sat on a winnock sole, and sang the king a bonny sang. And the king says to the queen: 'What'll we gie to wee Robin for singing us this bonny sang?' And the queen says to the king: 'I think we'll gie him the wee wran to be his wife.' So wee Robin and the wee wran were married, and the king, and the queen, and a' the court danced at the waddin'; syne he flew awa' hame to his ain water-side, and happit on a brier.

* * *

[The above little story is taken down from the recitation of Mrs Begg, the sister of Robert Burns. The poet was in the habit of telling it to the younger members of his father's house-hold, and Mrs Begg's impression is, that he *made* it for their amusement.]

~ *Robert Chambers* ~

ROBINETS AN JENNY WRENS
ARE GOD A'MICHTY'S COCKS AN HENS

UNGRATEFU JENNY

Jenny Wren fa'd seeck
Upon a canty time,
In cam Robin Reidbreist
An brocht her saps an wine.

'Eat weel o the saps, Jenny,
Drink weel o the wine.'
'Thank ye Robin, kindly,
Ye sall be mine.'

Jenny Wren gat weel
An stuid upon her feet;
An telt Robin plainlike
She loed him deil a haet.

Robin he grew gurly,
An happit on a brod,
Sayin, 'Oot upon ye,
  ... fegs upon ye,
Bauld-gizzed jaud!'

THE ROBINS

Robin Reidbreist an his son
Ance gaed tae toun tae buy a bun
They couldna gree on plum or plain.
Sae awa they gaed, back hame again.

A RIDDLE

I'm cried by the name o a chiel,
Yet am sma as a mous.
Whan winter comes I blythely bide
Wi' my reid terget inby the hous.

ANSWER: A robin

THE NOR WIND

The Nor Wind doth blaw
An we sall hae snaw
An what will puir Robin dae then,
Puir thing?
He'll sit in the barn
An keep hissel warm,
An haud his heid under his wing,
Puir thing.

~ *Traditional;* owerset by *Marjory Greig* ~

WELCOME LITTLE ROBIN

Welcome, little robin
With the scarlet breast
In this wintry weather
Cold must be your nest.
Hopping o'er the carpet
Picking up the crumbs
Robin knows the children
Welcome when he comes.

Is the story true, robin
You were once so good
To the little orphans
Sleeping in the wood?
Did you see them lying
Cold and pale and still
And strew leaves about them
With your little bill?

~ *Anon* ~

NEW BOOTS FOR SANTA

ONCE upon a time, perhaps it was only yesterday, or maybe it was the day before, Santa Claus sat in a little house in the middle of the A–Z Family Stores. Icicles hung from the roof of Santa's little house. When the fairy lights turned green, the icicles turned green, and when somebody came in at the door with a 'whoosh', the icicles shivered and went 'klik, klak, klik, klak, klik'. When the fairy lights turned red, the icicles turned red, and when somebody went out at the door with a 'whoosh', the icicles shivered and went 'klak, klik, klak, klik, klak'.

Santa sat inside his little house and worried and listened to the icicles kliking and klaking outside. Santa was worried because his boots weren't fit to be seen. It was no wonder, really, for Santa had been wearing his boots for as long as he could remember. Which was a very long time indeed, for Santa Claus has a very long memory. Of course, it would be easy to buy a new pair of boots. Come to think of it, there was a pair right in the middle of the A–Z's plate-glass window – long, shiny red boots, with a border of soft white fur round their tops. But Santa had no money to buy such beautiful boots, for he had spent every penny he possessed on presents for other people.

Santa looked at his reflection in one of the icicles that kliked outside the window. 'Oh, you're a very shabby old Santa indeed,' he scolded. 'Holes in your socks and holes in your mittens. And those dreadful old boots.' He groaned. He might get away with the darns in his coat, only his toes knew about the holes in his socks, and he could always take off his mittens.

'But you can't hide your boots,' Santa told himself. 'Doesn't matter whether you come in at the window or go out at the door – or – or – drop down somebody's chimney. Ten to one it's your boots people see first – or last – depending on whether they happen to see you coming or going.'

Just then a sparrow flew in at the open window. 'Doesn't matter what you look like,' said the sparrow. 'It's their presents they care about. They wouldn't care if the coalman came down the chimney. It's what's in the sack that counts.'

'D'you really think so?' asked Santa. 'You really think it wouldn't matter who delivered their presents?'

'Of course it wouldn't,' said the sparrow. 'It's the presents they care about.' And away he flew.

A tear trickled down Santa's cheek and landed on his beard. 'And I always thought that Santa Claus was part of Christmas,' he said.

Just then a robin flew in at the window. 'What's this? What's this? Christmas without Santa? Coalmen delivering presents. They wouldn't like that at all.'

'Well,' said Santa. 'I know I'm a perfect sight. I just can't go delivering presents in these old boots.' He hesitated. 'Well, at least, I thought I couldn't. But, of course, if you think the coalman ....'

'Oh nonsense,' said the robin. He flew on to the top of the window. 'Now let's see. What kind of boots?'

Santa sighed. 'Long, red, shiny boots, with – with a border of soft white fur round their tops,' he said wistfully.

'Gosh,' gasped robin. 'Right! Be back in half an hour.' And off he flew, setting the icicles kliking and klaking outside the window. And in half an hour robin was back, but this time he wasn't alone. Dozens and dozens of robins came flying in at the open window of Santa's little house and settled on the chairs, on the picture frames and on the mantelpiece. Each robin held in his beak a bright red holly berry. One by one the robins flew on to the table and began beating the holly berries flat with their beaks. Sometimes a greedy robin would stop and swallow the little seed inside the holly berry.

'What in the world are you doing?' asked Santa.

'You'll see,' sang the robins as they beat and beat the holly berries flat. And they puffed out their scarlet breasts and sang, to the tune of 'The farmer wants a wife':

> Holly berry boots,
> Holly berry boots,
> Santa's in your chimney
> In holly berry boots.
>
> No fancy mittens,
> No fancy suits,
> He'll come down your chimney
> In holly berry boots.

With all this singing going on, Santa began to feel quite cheerful again and, after a while, he joined in the chorus:

> Holly berry boots,
> Holly berry boots,
> Santa's in your chimney
> In holly berry boots.

Soon the table was covered with hundreds and hundreds of bright red holly berry skins. One of the robins had a tape measure hanging round his neck and he began to measure Santa's feet.

'Oh dearie dearie me,' he sang. 'Size elevens.' Then, as he measured the length of Santa's leg, he sang, 'Oh dearie, dearie me. Twenty-seven inches! That's a very large pair of holly berry boots.'

'That's going to take an awful lot of holly berry skins,' chirped another.

When all the berries were beaten flat, the robins sewed them together with pine needles and fine grasses. They were the finest boots you could imagine – long and shiny and red. Santa could see his face in them. He began to pull them on.

'Wait a minute,' chirped a robin. 'We've forgotten something. We've forgotten the white fur round their tops.'

'They're beautiful enough without the fur,' said Santa. 'I'll wear them just as they are.'

'No! No!' said the robins. 'You wanted white tops and everybody gets what they want at Christmas.'

'Except Santa Claus,' sang another. 'Nobody bothers about poor old Santa. They're all too busy asking for what *they* want.'

'But what can we use for white tops?' asked a third.

All the robins thought very hard. It was very quiet in the little house except for the noise the icicles made outside.

'I know,' chirped a robin. 'We'll hang a fringe of icicles round Santa's boots.'

So the robins flew outside and broke off the white icicles. They looked beautiful round the tops of Santa's boots. And when Santa moved they made a lovely silvery kliking sound.

Santa was so pleased, because now he was able to deliver your presents after all. He knew you wouldn't really like a coal man to take his place, at Christmas. I wonder, did you hear the icicles go klik, klak, klik last night? And did you hear the robins singing:

> Holly berry boots,
> Holly berry boots,
> Santa's in your chimney
> In holly berry boots.

~ Marjorie Wilson ~

A RIDDLE

Hichty, tichty, paradichty,
Cled a in green
The king couldna read it,
Nae mair could the queen.
They sent for the Wyss Men
Oot o the East
They said it had horns,
But wisna a beast.

ANSWER: A holly leaf

~ *Traditional;* owerset by *Marjory Greig* ~

THE BUBBLY-JOCK

I've feasted late an' I've feasted early –
Nae scrimpit meals for the turkey-cock –
But I jalouse they've begunked me fairly,
A weird to dree has the bubbly-jock.

I've fattened sae that my sides are hingin',
A wee thing mair an' I couldna walk;
Noo a voice o' doom in my lug is ringin':
'When'll we kill the bubbly-jock?'

Sae that's the wey o' it! Yuletide's comin'.
Haverin' hypocrites, hear them talk:
Peace an' guidwill to men an' women –
But thraw the neck o' the bubbly-jock!

I've fleyed the hens an' the jucks richt rudely
Frichit the grumphie frae his brock,
Ruled the roost like a king gey proodly –
A dooncome this for the bubbly-jock!

I've garred the tinkler's weans rin greetin',
Gi'ed the gangerels mony a shock:
Watch-dougs wouldna be killed for eatin' –
Why the de'il should a bubbly-jock!

Man's ingratitude! Noo they've catched me!
Gie me smeddum to thole this shock!
Waesome day when my mither hatched me!
Here's fareweel to the bubbly-jock!

~ *W D Cocker* ~

HEN'S LAMENT

It's nae delight tae be a hen
Wi' clooks an claws an caimb.
Reestin wi the rottans
In a hen-hoose for a hame.

Nae suner div I sattle doon,
My clutch o' bairns tae hatch
The fairm-wife comes – a scraunin' pest –
She cowps me aff ma cosy nest
A tarry-fingered vratch.

Jist lately, though, she's changed her tune –
Ma platie's piled wi' corn,
'Sup up, ma bonnie quine,' says she,
'We're haein broth the morn!'

~ Sheena Blackhall ~

CHRISTMAS IS COMIN

Christmas is comin
The geese are growin fat
Please tae pit a bawbee in
The auld bodach's hat.
Gin ye haena gotten a bawbee
A bodle will dae.
Gin ye haena gotten a bodle
The Lord sain ye!

~ Traditional; owerset by *Marjory Greig ~*

From ELEGY ON LUCKY WOOD

She gae us aft hale legs o' lamb,
And didna hain her mutton ham;
Then aye at Yule whene'er we cam',
    A braw gooose-pie:
An' wasna that good belly-baum?
    Nane dare deny.

~ Allan Ramsay ~

ON CHRISTMAS EVE

On Christmas Eve I caa'd the spit,
I brunt ma finger, I find it yet
The wee cock speug flew ower the table,
The pat begoud tae jeuk wi the ladle.

~ Traditional; owerset by *Marjory Greig ~*

FEATHER FOWLIE
(An Old Scots Chicken Soup)

1 plump fowl	1 dessertspoonful chopped parsley
A slice of ham	salt
A pot posy:	pepper
2 sprigs parsley	1 quart water
1 sprig thyme	1 ladleful first stock
1 blade mace	2-3 egg yolks
1 onion (medium)	1 dessertspoonful cream
1 stick celery	

Joint the fowl, and let the pieces soak for half an hour in water to cover, with a dessertspoonful of salt; then wash well and put into a stew pan with the ham, chopped celery, sliced onion, herbs, and water. Cover, and bring to the boil; then draw to the side and cook gently for 1½ hours. Strain, and remove all grease. Return the soup to the rinsed pan, and add the stock. Heat it up for fifteen minutes, then add the parsley and some of the minced white meat of the fowl. Remove from the fire, stir in the strained egg yolks and the warmed cream, and pour into a heated tureen.

The remainder of the fowl may be served with egg or parsley or bread sauce and curled rashers of bacon, or it may be made into patties.

~ F Marian McNeill ~

FOR A GOOSE-PYE

THE PASTRY:

Take 2 lib of Butter, and a Peck of Flour, melt the Butter in boiling Water, and work it very well for all sorts of raised Paste: For cold Paste, take 3 lib and a half of Butter for each Peck of Flour, and wet the Flour with cold Water, then roll in your Butter. For Puff-paste, for each Peck of Flour, take 4 lib and a half of sweet Butter, and the Whites of 4 Eggs and beat them a little, take a little of the Flour and mix with the Eggs and cold Water, and work them well together, till it come to a Paste thick for rolling out, then roll it out, put in flour beneath that it may not stick to the Table, and put on the Butter, strawing a handful of Flour over the Butter, then fold it together and roll it out 6 or 7 times, always strewing Flour upon it every time it is rolled out, and so apply it to the Use you design.

THE FILLING:

Break the Bones of the Goose, and rub it within and without with black Spice, Jamaica Pepper, and Nutmeg, lay it in the Pye, with the Giblets round about the Goose, to fill up the Corners of the Pye, give it a good store of Butter, Spice, Salt, then put on the lid, and send it to the Oven.

TO MAKE LIQUOR FOR THE PYE:

Take half a Mutchkin of white Wine with a Lemon squeezed. Take the Yolk of 3 Eggs, mix all together, and put it in the Pye when it comes out of the Oven.

~ Mrs McLintock ~

APPLE SAUCE

1 lb apples	$^1/_2$ oz butter
1 gill water	$^1/_2$ oz sugar

Peel, core and slice the apples. Put into a saucepan with the water, butter and sugar and cook until quite soft. Beat smooth with the back of a wooden spoon, or rub through a hair sieve, and reheat.

~ Edinburgh College of Domestic Science ~

RED CABBAGE TO PICKLE

Take a firm cabbage, wash well and take off outside leaves. Shred cabbage into slender slips and place a layer on a sieve, and sprinkle it freely with salt. Repeat till all is salted. Allow to remain two days thus, turning several times to drain, then put in jar. Boil 1 pint vinegar with 1 teaspoonful peppercorns, 6 cloves, a blade of mace, one cooked and pulped cooking apple and pour the mixture hot over the cabbage. A few slices of beetroot will improve the colour. When cold, cover up tightly.

~ Mrs E W Kirk ~

SAVOURY POTATOES

8 large potatoes	$^1/_2$ pint water
1 large onion	1 teaspoonful sage
2 oz butter	salt and pepper

Pare potatoes and slice them; chop onion fine; grease a pie dish. Put a layer of potatoes, sprinkle pepper and salt, sage and onions. Place butter in pieces on the top. Add water and bake for 1$^1/_4$ hours.

~ Mrs E W Kirk ~

CHRISTMAS COMES

Christmas comes but ance a year,
An whan it comes, it brings guid cheer:
A pouchfu o siller, a cellarfu o beer,
An a guid swak grice tae lest ye aa the year.

~ Traditional; owerset by *Marjory Greig ~*

AN INVITATION

'IT'S frae Mistress Purdie,' said Lizzie, handing the letter which she had just perused to her husband, who was reading his paper and smoking his pipe in the fullness of contentment in front of the kitchen fire.

'Dod,' exclaimed John, grinning as he examined the envelope, 'But yer guid-sister's gettin' up in the warl' wi' her fancy paper an' mauve ink. Whit's she writin' ye aboot?'

'Luk at the inside, an ye'll see. I wis expectin' the letter, fur I seen her yesterday, an' she tell't me it wis comin'.'

John extracted a gilt-edged card from the envelope. 'Whit's a' this, whit's a' this?' he cried, staring at the card, upon which was written in bright purple the following:

Mr and Mrs Robert Purdie
requests the pleasure of
Mr and Mrs ROBINSON's
company for dinner on
Thursday evening, 25th December,
at 7 o'clock p.m.

John read it through aloud, and then gaped at his wife …. 'At seeven o'clock! ….'

'Tits, man! …. Can ye no' see we're askit to a Christmas dinner?'

'Oh, that's it, is't?' And John burst into a great guffaw.

'I dinna see muckle to lauch aboot,' his wife said a little impatiently ….

'You an' me, wumman, askit to a Christmas dinner! Haw, haw, haw! ….'

'Ay,' said Lizzie shortly ….

'Dod, but her an' her man are the gentry noo! No' but whit it wisna unco kind o' them to ask us yins to their pairty. But I doot we'll no' be able to eat muckle sae shin efter wur tea.'

'Aw, we'll jist miss wur tea that nicht, John,' said Lizzie, recovering her good humour. 'Fur Mistress Purdie tell't me she wis gaun to gi'e us a graun' dinner – soup, an' a turkey wi' sassingers roon' aboot, an' ploom puddin', an' pies, an' frit furbye.'

'I'm thinkin' ye wud be as weel to get a botle o' yer ile ready fur me, Lizzie, for this day week,' he observed jocularly. 'But whit wey is yer guid-sister no' ha'ein' her pairty at Ne'erday?'

'Aweel, John, she thinks it's mair genteel-like to haud Christmas …. I wudna like to refuse to gang to the pairty. An' I'm rale gled ye're pleased aboot it.'

'I didna say I wis pleased aboot it, wumman, fur I'm no' up to gentry weys,' said John seriously. Then he suddenly brightened as his son entered the kitchen. 'Here he comes wi' as mony feet 's a hen!' he cried merrily. 'Come awa,' Macgreegor, an gi'e's yer crack ....'

'Wullie's maw bakit tawtie scones fur wur tea,' returned Macgregor.

'Did she that? Aweel, ye'll be gettin' mair nor scones this time next week, ma mannie! Ye'll be gettin' turkeys, an' pies, an' sassingers, an' terts, an' orangers, an' – '

'Whisht, man, whisht!' cried Lizzie in dire dismay.

'Och, it's nae hairm tellin' Macgreegor aboot the guid things he'll be gettin' at his Aunt – '

'Is't a pairty, Paw?' asked Macgregor delightedly.

'Deed, ay! Yer Aunt Purdie's gaun to dae the thing in style! It's to be a rale high-class Christmas denner! Whit think ye o' that?'

'John, John!' broke out the unhappy Lizzie. 'Ye've done it noo!'

'Whit ha'e I done, dearie?' her husband asked in amazement.

'I'll tell ye efter. But, fur mercy's sake, dinna cheep anither word aboot the pairty the noo.'

'Vera weel, wumman,' said John, in a state of complete bewilderment.

'Is turkeys guid fur eatin', Paw?' inquired Macgregor ....

'We'll no' heed aboot turkey the noo. Yer Maw's feart ye'll dream aboot bubbly-jocks an' sassingers till ye think ye've ett dizzens, an' then she'll be fur gi'ein' ye ile.' John patted his son's head, and tried to laugh, but failed.

'I'm awfu' gled we're gaun to the pairty,' said Macgregor.

'Ay, ay,' said his father. 'But keep quate fur a wee, an' I'll tell ye a story.'

The story was of sufficient interest to keep the youngster from the tabooed subject till bedtime, but when his mother was tucking him in he murmured sleepily:

'I – I'll behave masel' awfu' weel at Aunt Purdie's pairty, Maw.'

'Aw, wee Macgreegor!' whispered Lizzie ....

With a lump in her throat she returned to her husband, and regarded him reproachfully.

'John, John,' she said at last. 'Wull ye never be discreet? Ye kent fine Macgreegor canna gang to the pairty.'

'No' gang to the pairty?' He sat up, staring at her. 'Whit fur no'?'

'Jist because he wisna askit.'

'But – but Macgreegor likes pairties!'

'But I tell ye, Macgreegor wisna askit.'

John's countenance turned very red. 'An' whit wey wis he no' askit?' he demanded, almost fiercely.

'Oh, man, man, it's no' the thing fur a wean ava .... I wud be gey sweirt to let him gang. But noo I dinna ken whit to dae. Ye've tell't the wean he's to gang, an' – an' he canna gang.'

'Ach, he can gang fine, Lizzie. He'll no' eat that muckle. Ye can easy tell her we're bringin' Macgreegor.'

'Wud ye ha'e me affrontit, John?' cried Lizzie.

'Toots, havers! She kens fine, onywey, we wudna gang wantin' Macgreegor. Deed, ay! that'll be the reason she didna fash to write his name on the caird ....'

Lizzie shook her head mournfully. 'They tell me ye're unco smairt at yer wark, John, an' maybe that's enough for a man; but – but – aweel, *I* daursay ye dae yer best.' She heaved a great sigh and took up her knitting.

A minute passed ere John said slowly: 'Did yer guid-sister say we *wisna* to bring Macgreegor?'

After some hesitation Lizzie replied: 'She jist said she supposed we wudna be feart to leave him in the hoose that nicht, an' I tell't her I had nae doot I wud get Mistress M'Faurlan to bide wi' him.'

'Aw, I see ... I see,' said John thoughtfully. 'She supposed we wudna be feart to leave him in the hoose, did she suppose? .... I tell ye whit it is, wumman ... she didna want Macgreegor!'

'Tits! Ye needna flee up like that, John,' said his wife. 'Ye're fair rideec'lous aboot Macgreegor ... '

'Ye needna say anither word, Lizzie ... I'll no' pit a foot inside yer guid-sister's door fur a' the turkeys, an' sassingers, an' snashters in creation! I'm jist tellin' ye!' And John rose abruptly, caught up his cap, and stalked from the kitchen and out of the house.

When he returned, half-an-hour later, he was calm, but absolutely firm in his determination not to be present at the Purdies' Christmas dinner.

'Them as disna want Macgreegor disna want me.'

'My! But ye're a dour yin!' Lizzie said at last. 'Hoo dae ye ken Mistress Purdie disna want Macgreegor?'

'She aye had a spite at the wean; an' fine ye ken it!' he retorted.

Lizzie wavered .... 'I wudna ha'e let Macgreegor gang, even if he had been askit,' she said, after a pause. 'He's ower young, an' he needs haudin' doon instead o' bein' pit furrit afore his elders. But ... oh, John, I'm vexed fur the wean, fur he'll be that disappintit. Oh, I wisht ye hadna said onythin' aboot the pairty.'

'Deed, Lizzie, I wisht I hadna,' admitted John despondently ....

'Ye'll jist ha'e to tell him we're no gaun to the pairty efter a',' said Lizzie.

'Wud ye no' gang yersel', dearie?'

'John!'

'Weel, I thocht ye wis set on the pairty.'

'Ach, John, ye ken fine I thocht you wud like it .... I'll jist ha'e to tell her we canna gang. But whit aboot Macgreegor? Wull *you* tell him, John?'

'Na, na! Never let bug to Macgreegor there's to be nae pairty till I can mak' up some ither treat fur him,' said John, beginning to recover his spirits.

'Whit kin' o' a treat?'

'Och, I'll tell ye when I get it a' arranged.'

'John, ye're no' to gang an' be wasterfu',' said Lizzie warningly. 'Wud it no' be best jist to tell him he'll get his treat at Ne'erday?'

'I'll see, I'll see,' replied her husband. 'But never let bug aboot the pairty till I tell ye. Promise, dearie.'

Lizzie promised reluctantly, and John lit his pipe … and smoked steadily for the next ten minutes without speaking a word.

'But whit am I to write to Mistress Purdie?' inquired Lizzie ….

'Oh,' said her husband with a chuckle, 'jist say we're vexed we canna gang to her pairty, because Macgreegor's ha'ein' a pairty o' his ain that night.'

'Ma word, John!' said Lizzie, and proceeded to ask questions to which she got no answers.

* * *

The next day, Friday, John was exceedingly thoughtful.

On Saturday he was grave; on Sunday he was unusually glum. On Monday he was distinctly irritable and nervous; and on Tuesday he was wrapped in gloom. But on Wednesday he came home to his dinner in a state of repressed excitement and his wife made many inquiries without receiving any satisfaction. At tea he burst out into frequent guffaws without apparent reason.

'Macgreegor's talkin' aboot naethin' but his Aunt Purdie's pairty the morn's nicht,' said Lizzie, in an undertone, as she started to clear away the dishes.

'Dod, he'll get his pairty,' he returned.

'Man, man,' she whispered … 'whit's his treat to be? Tell me noo, John.'

But he laughed, and rose from the table, and put on his cap. 'Here, Macgreegor, come ootbye fur a dauner,' he cried.

* * *

Father and son returned about eight o'clock.

Macgregor came first up the stair, panting and puffing with excitement and exhaustion; John followed, chuckling.

They took breath before John softly turned his key in the door. Then they crept into the little house like a pair of burglars.

Lizzie was sitting by the kitchen fire when the door flew open and her son tottered in, screaming with laughter, tripped, and fell, with a squelch, on something soft. He rose at once, still screaming with laughter, and the something soft was seen to be a medium-sized turkey. Macgregor picked it up and dumped it into his astounded mother's lap. Then John entered … bearing sundry parcels ….

'John,' Lizzie cried, 'ye've been at the savings bank the day!'

But John laid his parcels on the dresser and went close to his wife. 'Haud the turkey, Macgreegor,' he said and then began to whisper to her.

'Ye're jist jokin'!' cried Lizzie after a minute's whispering.

'As shair's daith!' said John.

She gave a short sob. 'They've really made ye foreman at the works, John!'

'Jist that.'

'But ye micht hae tell't me shinner.'

'I didna like. Ye see … I never thocht o' speirin' aboot the place till last Thursday …. But somewey I thocht then I wud like mair cash fur yersel … an' Macgreegor. An' I says to masel': "Naethin' bates a trial" …. An' I tried, wumman …. An' I got the place … I'm foreman efter the holidays …. Ye'll no be angry if I tell ye it wis the thocht o' Macgreegor's pairty that gie'd me the neck to try fur the place …. But the pairty's for us yins, an naebody else, fur I'm no haudin' wi' Christmas – as a rule …. Are ye pleased, Lizzie?'

Lizzie nodded, speechless.

'Paw,' said Macgregor, 'come on an' ha'e a scud at wur turkey. It's fine fun skelpin' it.'

~ J J Bell ~

A CHRISTMAS DINNER MENU

CLEAR SOUP

2 or 3 lb shin of beef
1 turnip
2 carrots
A leek

A little celery
egg-shells
some peppercorns

Cut meat off bones, and take out the marrow. Put bones and meat in pan; cover with cold water, and bring slowly to boil. Skim well. When it boils, put in the vegetables and some egg-shells, and a few peppercorns, tied in a bit of muslin. Draw pan to the side, and let it simmer for 5 or 6 hours; do not put the lid on. Strain through a dish napkin. Care must be taken that it does not boil quickly, or it will look muddy.

~ Mrs E W Kirk ~

ROASTIT BUBBLY-JOCK

1 hen turkey, 12-14 lb
chestnut and oyster stuffing (see below)
sausagemeat stuffing (see below)
salt and pepper to taste

Wash and dry bird. Rub the inside with salt. Fill crop lightly with chestnut and oyster stuffing, then fold the skin over onto the back and skewer or sew in place. Stuff body with sausage meat and sew up or skewer opening or close it with a heel of stale bread. Truss and weigh. Place bird on one side on rack in a roasting tin. Brush all over with melted butter or chicken fat. Cover with a piece of butter muslin dipped in melted fat. Roast, uncovered, in a slow oven, 300°F, until tender, allowing about 20 minutes per lb. Baste every $1/2$ hour with drippings in pan and turn at the same time on its other side, so that the bird cooks evenly. When half cooked, sprinkle all over with salt and pepper or paprika to taste. Remove muslin $1/2$ hour before dishing up and turn bird on its back. Baste well, and continue to cook until evenly browned. Untruss. Dish up. Garnish with watercress, and bacon and mushroom rolls, and paper frills. Serve with brown gravy, bread sauce, green peas and roast potatoes.

CHESTNUT AND OYSTER STUFFING:

> 1 pint sieved boiled chestnuts
> ¹/₂ cup melted butter or margarine
> 1 small teaspoon salt, pepper to taste
> ¹/₄ cup top milk
> 1 cup dry breadcrumbs
> 2 tablespoons chopped parsley
> ¹/₂ cup chopped celery
> 1 tablespoon grated onion
> 1 pint small oysters

Mix the chestnut puree with all the fat except 2 tablespoons, salt, pepper, top milk, crumbs, parsley, celery and onion. Chop the oysters, and simmer for 2 minutes in the remainder of the melted fat and add.

SAUSAGEMEAT STUFFING:

> 2¹/₂ lb pork sausage meat
> minced fried turkey liver
> salt and cayenne pepper to taste
> 1 tablespoon minced onion
> ¹/₄ teaspoon crushed herbs.

Mix ingredients together till blended.

BACON AND MUSHROOM ROLLS:

Allow 1 rasher of thin streaky bacon and 2 small peeled mushrooms per person. Halve the rashers. Roll a mushroom up in each portion, and run on the skewer. Grill slowly till bacon is crisp.

BROWN GRAVY:

Pour off all the drippings from pan except 1¹/₂ tablespoons. Sprinkle in 3 teaspoons flour, then stir in about ³/₄ pint giblet stock. Bring to boil, stirring constantly, then season with salt and freshly-ground pepper and add a dash of gravy browning if necessary.

CRANBERRY SAUCE:

1 lb sound cranberries   2 teacups water
¾ lb granulated sugar

Pick over and wash cranberries in a colander under the cold water tap. Drain thoroughly. Place berries, sugar and water in a saucepan. Bring to boil. Cover. Simmer for about 10 minutes till skins all break, then skim and cool. Pour into sterilised small pots and seal. Use as required. This will make about 1½ lb of sauce.

~ Elizabeth Craig ~

BOILED CARROTS

Wash and scrape the carrots, and, if they are large, cut them in half, lengthwise and across. Put them in a pan of boiling salted water and boil for one hour till soft. Drain, dish, and coat with a white sauce; or toss in melted butter, dish neatly, and sprinkle with finely chopped parsley.

BRUSSELS SPROUTS au JUS

1 lb brussels sprouts
1 pint stock

Trim and wash the sprouts and cook for five minutes in boiling salted water. Drain, and put them into the boiling stock. Cook till tender, about twenty minutes, dish neatly; reduce the stock by quick boiling, and pour it round the sprouts.

~ Edinburgh College of Domestic Science

CASSEROLE OF POTATOES

Take 1½ lb mashed potatoes, add salt, pepper, ½ oz butter and ½ egg. Mix all well; flour a board and form it into a cake with pyramid in centre. Put it on a greased baking-tin; brush it over with the other ½ egg and bake ½ hour. Place sausages round it.

~ Mrs E W Kirk ~

BOSTON CREAM

[I have only met this beverage in Scotland … though its name does not suggest a Scottish origin.]

2 lemons
3 quarts boiling water
1 1/2 lb sugar

2 oz tartaric acid
3 egg whites

Wash and dry lemons. Peel thinly. Place the peel with the lemon juice in a basin. Add water, acid and sugar. Stir till sugar is dissolved. When quite cold, stir in the beaten egg whites. Bottle. When required, dilute to taste with chilled soda water.

~ Elizabeth Craig ~

GRANNY'S PLUM PUDDING

1 lb each suet, currants, sultanas, raisins
bread crumbs
1/2 lb mixed peel
1/4 lb sugar
8 eggs
brandy or whisky to moisten

Chop suet finely and mix all dry ingredients. Add eggs one by one, and enough brandy to make mixture moist but not too wet. Put into floured cloth, and when tying up leave enough room for ingredients to swell. Boil six hours without ceasing. Serve with caudle sauce.

CAUDLE SAUCE:

Beat well together 4 oz butter and 4 oz sugar. Add half wine glass of brandy or rum, and a little cinnamon on top.

~ Scottish Women's Rural Institutes ~

PLUM DUFF

Flour o' Scotland, fruit o' Spain
Trysted thegither in a shour o' rain,
Rowed up in a cloot, tied roun wi string.
Gin ye tell me this riddle
I'll gie ye a ring!

~ Traditional; owerset by Marjory Greig ~

CRY YULE

Yule, Yule, Yule,
Three puddings in a pule!
Crack nuts and cry Yule!

~ Traditional ~

HEY FOR SUNDAY

Hey for Sunday
At twal o'clock,
Whan aa the plum puddens
Loup oot o the pot!

~ Traditional; owerset by Marjory Greig ~

TRIFLE

6 or 8 stale sponge cakes
3 gills custard
$^1/_2$ gill sherry
strawberry jam
glacé fruits, chopped nuts to decorate

juicy fresh or bottled fruit
3 or 4 bananas
1 oz ratafia biscuits
$^1/_2$ pint double cream

Slice sponge cakes thinly and spread with jam. Arrange in layers in a glass dish. Pour sherry over, adding fruit juice if desired. Make custard. Add a layer of sliced bananas and pour hot custard over, keeping back one third. Put fruit on top, and add remaining custard. When cold, put whipped, sweetened cream on top and decorate.

~ Scottish Women's Rural Institutes ~

MOONSHINE

1 oz gelatine
$^1/_4$ lb sugar

1 pint boiling water
2 lemons

Dissolve gelatine in a little cold water. Add boiling water and sugar, also the grated rind of the lemons. Boil for $^1/_4$ hour. Strain and add the juice of two lemons. When nearly cold, whisk till it is snow-white. Set till next day. Turn out and decorate with silver balls.

~ Mrs E W Kirk ~

A CHRISTMAS DISH FOR THE BAIRNS

Prepare some packet jellies; take as many oranges as required and make them into baskets by taking two pieces off the top, leaving a strip across for a handle. Remove the inside which can be quartered, and place on a glass dish. Fill the baskets with the prepared jelly. Place in a nice dish and ornament with holly or green leaves.

~ Mrs E W Kirk ~

CHRISTMAS BLUES

Chap the tatties, bree the neeps,
Gie the broth a steer,
Dicht the bairnie's faces,
Christmas denner's here!
Clootie dumplin in the pan,
Hotterin up an doon,
Fairy lights gyang 'Punk' again!
Haun the tangies roun,
Birsled bubbly jock fur wiks,
Halflins scalin beer,
Balloons that winna bide up,
An sotter on the fleer!
Faither squar-eed watchin sport,
Littlins wint cartoons,
They've riven oot the aerial.
Fa inventit loons?
Still, it's ainly aince a year,
Fit's that, I hear ye say?
Clear the table o mineer
Roll on Hogmanay?

~ Sheena Blackhall ~

CHRISTMAS CONTRAST

On Christmas day we hae a feast
Fit for the Wise Men frae the east …
Big clootie-dumplin' decked wi' holly,
Trifles an' jogglie jeelies jolly,
Veggies can keep their meatless stew –
We've chicken, lamb, an' turkey too.
(Sma' winder Santa's robes were red
Wi' a' the bluid that had been shed.)

In Bangladesh a wee bit lad
Grat for the mait that nane o's had;
Yowled for some rice the morn tae see,
But nane had onie rice tae gie.
For him nae joy or Christmas cheer,
His close companions – hunger, fear.
(Whan will oor red-robed Santa kind
Keep Bangladesh broon bairns in mind?)

~ Jamie A Smith ~

CAROL FOR THE HANDICAPPED

Little Jesus, perfect child
    In body and in mind,
Bless and help the ones to whom
    Life has not been kind;
Children who must face the world
    Lame or deaf or blind.
Grant that they on Christmas Day,
    Happiness may find.

~ Prue Guild ~

PRAYER FOR CHRISTMAS NIGHT

O God, our Father, we thank Thee for the happiness of this Christmas Day.
For the presents we have received; for the happiness we have enjoyed; for the meals
we have eaten together, the games we have played together, the talk we have
had together,

We thank Thee, O God.

We thank Thee for the peace and goodwill which have been amongst us all today.
Grant that they may not be something which lasts only for today; but grant that
we may take the Christmas joy and the Christmas fellowship with us into all the
ordinary days of life.

Now at evening time we specially remember those for whom Christmas has not
been a happy time. Bless those to whom sorrow came, and for whom it was all
the sorer, because it came at the time when everyone else was so happy. Bless those
who have no friends, no homes, no family circle, no one to remember them; and
be with them in their loneliness to comfort and to cheer them. O God, we thank
Thee for today; help us to try to deserve all our happiness a little more. Through
Jesus Christ our Lord. Amen.

~ William Barclay ~

THE FORGOTTEN
CHILDREN OF BETHLEHEM

It was Moussa Abuakere (76) who directed me to the village of
orphans.

He sells rosary beads on the doorstep of the Church of the Nativity in
Bethlehem.

The entrance to the manger is his shelter. It's also his livelihood.

He'd probably starve without the birthplace of Christ. It provides him
with shekels to survive the cold winter.

When I approached him he was huddled alone in a dark alcove of the
altar, sheltering from the cold and rain.

In Scotland we'd call him a tramp. In Bethlehem he is a wise man. I sat listening to his tales and prophecies.

He told me many stories, including one about a shepherd east of Bethlehem who wears a kilt to keep him warm in the hills.

There are many yarns about this mysterious kiltie shepherd. I'd even heard he plays the bagpipes to call in his flock.

Moussa told me the shepherd's village was Kisan, 20 kilometres from Bethlehem along dangerous desert tracks.

An Arab taxi driver offered to take me there for 100 shekels (£25). We passed refugee camps. Packs of wild dogs chased the taxi. We were stoned by Arab youths, their faces hidden behind kaffiyehs.

I arrived at the village of Kisan in search of the mysterious shepherd.

What I found was a heart-rending scene of starvation and desperation. A human tragedy at the very heart of Christianity.

Bare-footed children sat crying and shivering. They wore only light T-shirts, yet an icy wind howled in from the desert.

It seemed a village full of children. Hardly an adult in sight.

Yet some still managed a smile. They sat on the rubble which used to be their homes. The soldiers, they said, had destroyed them.

The winter winds have brought fever and death here.

The shepherds' children are the forgotten babies of Bethlehem. I'll never forget their example.

They showed no bitterness, only love. They didn't understand greed. Only giving.

I offered them chocolate from a Christmas stocking I'd brought. They didn't know what it was – they'd never seen chocolate before.

An old shepherd approached me. He used to have 60 sheep, now he has five.

Bassam Hassan (70) says the Israelis tried to clear them from the land to make way for modern Jewish settlements.

There used to be 600 villagers. Now there are 60. The children are Bassam's only flock.

The kiltie shepherd? Yes, he used to live in Kisan.

His name was Nidal. He traded a lamb for his kilt in Bethlehem one Christmas.

He bought it from the Bethlehem Scouts, a Christian group who used to parade through Manger Square.

He'd also bought small bagpipes from the Scouts, and played them by an open fire in the village.

He's dead now. Bassam says he was shot. Villagers found him beside his flock, still clutching his shepherd's crook.

His little boy Achmad (3) lives in the village.

It's difficult to express the feelings I experienced when I turned my back on Kisan. Tragically there was little else I could do.

I make this promise. I will return to that village one day. To help.

~ From *The Sunday Post,* 1991 ~

THOUGHTS FOR YULE 1989

It's nae awfu fine
At Christmastime
When the banes are auld
An the hoose is cauld,
When ye're aa yer lane
Wi naebody there tae dunch the pain
O mindin on them as are deid an gane,
While the fowk ye loe bide faur frae hame.
It's an unco thing –
But the kirk bells ring
NOEL! NOEL!

It's nae awfu fine
At Christmastime
When ye're on the dole
An the bairnies greit
For ferlies wi prices ye canna meet;
Ye're owe the rent
Wi the siller spent,
An the wean wants shoon tae her feet.
Ye canna dae mair nor smile an thole.
It's no the thing –
But the kirk choirs bring
A NOEL! NOEL!

It's nae awfu fine
At Christmastime
When ye're a bit bairn, wantan an ee or a haun
Frae an eidant bomb in Afghanistan;
Or a laddie wi legs that winna ding
Throu a bullet that bieldit itsel in his spine,
In gurly, gilravaged Palestine.
It's an ill-trickit thing.
Hou can *we* sing –
NOEL! NOEL!

Noel? Noel?
Was it sae fine

That Christmastime,
In the cauld bare stable, lang, lang syne,
For the wee bit bairn cooried doun in the hay?
Wi nocht but the beasts tae gie him a heat,
An an orra cloot tae hap his feet;
An a life that wad tak him come what may
Tae a wuidden cross an a thorny croun.
But … wis there no a starn glinted doun
Frae the lift that nicht,
Lowed wi a hairt-warman, kindly licht,
An a promise that *ae* day wad daw a better thing?
Bairns, ye *maun* sing
NOEL! NOEL!

~ Marjory Greig ~

A BOXING DAY TO REMEMBER

NEVER shall I forget the nightmare journey we took on Boxing Day 1906. My father had conducted the Christmas service in Crathie Church, we had been absorbed in the usual lively party at the Manse, and had, as always, stayed overnight. It was snowing heavily when we left in the early afternoon, and a gale was blowing up. When the bus deposited us at the Gairn-side road-end the wind was so strong we could hardly remain upright. My father led the way, trying to shield us from the force of the wind, I followed at his heels, then came my mother sheltering Little Ellie in the folds of her cloak.

We ran into blin' drift; battling against it for less than two miles left us almost breathless. Our tired eyes peered into the white wilderness; we bent our heads to meet the frozen intensity of the wind which continually hurled great flurries of snow in our faces, and moved as if in a trance. Ballochrosk was not even half-way, but we were thankful to crave shelter there for a brief rest. It was the roadman's cottage. He and his wife were kindly and hospitable, and their children gazed in wonder at our Arctic appearance. Bedraggled and snow-encrusted, we relaxed at a blazing peat-fire, relishing mugs of scalding tea and thick slices of bread and jam. When the storm showed no signs of abating, we had to continue the struggle. By this time the high wind was forcing the snow into deep drifts. There was practically no visibility. Landmarks were blotted out and the blizzard raged on. The rest of that hazardous uphill journey is mercifully forgotten; we reached home safely, though almost exhausted. Lamps and a fire were lit in the cold, dark Manse, and, thawed at last, we tumbled thankfully into bed.

~ Amy Stewart Fraser ~

26th DECEMBER – SWEETIE SCONE DAY

In Scotland there is a custom of distributing sweet-cakes and a particular kind of sugared bread before and after the New Year.

~ From Gentlemen's Magazine, July 1790 ~

SCOTS CURRANT LOAF
(Old Family Recipe)

MAIN INGREDIENTS:

Flour, sugar, currants, raisins, orange peel, mixed spice, black pepper, ginger, cream of tartar, bicarbonate of soda, butter-milk (or fresh milk);

CRUST:

Flour, baking-powder, butter, water

Rub half a pound of butter into a pound and a half of flour. Add half a teaspoonful of baking-powder and mix to a paste with water. Roll out rather thinly and line a large cake-tin with the paste, reserving enough to cover the top.

Now put into a basin a pound of flour, half a pound of sugar, a pound of currants, washed and dried, half a pound of raisins, cleaned and stoned, a quarter-pound of orange peel, a teaspoonful of mixed spice, half a teaspoonful of ginger and the same of black pepper, one teaspoonful of bicarbonate of soda and one of cream of tartar. Just moisten with butter-milk. About a breakfast-cupful will be required. Complete as for Black Bun.

~ F Marian McNeill ~

THE CASTLE CELEBRATES

CHRISTMAS was another wonderful day. When my mother first came to the castle, she had been horrified to find that it was treated as an ordinary working day; she looked out of the window on the first Christmas morning of her marriage and was astounded to see the gardeners raking the gravel of the castle courtyard. Later in the day, she was amazed to discover the village shop open for trade and to find the blacksmith hammering noisily at an hour when she expected him to be on his knees in the kirk. The very next year, she set about importing the delights of Christmas, superimposing ... new customs on to rites that already existed ....

Finding that there was a tradition of feasting and decorating the castle with evergreen boughs, my mother had little difficulty in infiltrating turkeys, plum puddings and Christmas trees, and although everyone continued to work on Christmas Day, Christmas presents appeared – not only in the castle but all over the estate. My mother kept a reference book in which she had written down the names and birth dates of all the tenants' children and the presents that she had previously given them, and about a month before Christmas she would take us shopping to help her select the current year's gifts. Back home, dolls, footballs, clasp knives, mouth organs, toy soldiers, conjuring sets and other toys were laid out on the billiard table, labelled carefully, and tied up in holly-decked paper. My mother made it a rule never to give the children of the tenants anything useful, thinking that their lives were quite serious enough already. When all the parcels were done up, she would have them loaded into big wicker baskets and piled in the back of the Daimler; then she would set off around the estate. As she stopped for a chat at each house, this delivery of the presents could take anything up to a fortnight.

The best known of all the Scottish festivals, that of Hogmanay, was not celebrated in the castle, my father only acknowledging the existence of the New Year's Eve revelry by allowing, as was common all over Scotland, New Year's Day itself to be taken as a fully paid holiday.

Besides Christmas, my mother's other winter innovation was the hockey party. In those days, the lairds, even though they might be close friends with their tenants, did not mix with them socially, nor did they extend much of a welcome to local professional people. This resulted in an acute lack of companionship for their daughters. Whether these girls were home only for the holidays or ... living permanently in the widely separated castles, they rarely saw one another, and even more rarely had the chance of meeting young men .... Almost always, they were extremely lonely. My mother saw this and, trying to think of a way that a lot of young people could be entertained without too much trouble, hit on the idea of a hockey party. Hastening off to a school outfitter's, she bought several dozen hockey sticks. She then engaged the local band (one elderly lady who played the piano, accompanied by her son on the accordion), ordered in a large quantity of food, and sent out invitations.

From north, south, east and west, the young men and girls converged on the castle; those who were too young to drive were brought by their family chauffeurs, who were themselves glad of an outing. The young people arrived after lunch … and were at once sent out to the big lawn behind the castle to join whichever team had fewer players. There were no rules, no umpire, and no half-time – anybody who was exhausted simply dropped out, and rejoined his team when he felt better. Whoever arrived after all the hockey sticks had been appropriated used a golf club, a walking stick, or his foot. The scrimmage went on till dark, when everyone tumbled indoors to gorge on hot buttered scones and thick, spoon-supporting cocoa.

Then, while the servants busied themselves clearing away the tea and laying the table for dinner, the girls and young men went upstairs, where, strictly segregated, they had baths. The spare rooms allocated to the girls were littered with discarded pullovers and muddy shoes; party dresses hung from curtain rails and cupboard doors, petticoats were flung over chairs, and a confusion of evening slippers and embroidered handbags lay jumbled on the sofas. Under the eiderdowns of the huge beds, laughing, gossiping groups of girls – supposed to be resting – hugged their knees and chattered ….

At seven o'clock, the dressing gong boomed, and an hour later everyone was gathered in the dining room, where extra chairs had been crammed round all the tables. In the light of the flickering candles, the faces of the fifty or sixty young people who were seated at dinner glowed with excitement ….

In the Big Drawing Room, my mother had fixed a looking glass behind each of the wall brackets, so that it appeared that the room was lit by a hundred candles instead of fifty. Fires blazed in the fireplaces, the long curtains were tightly drawn … the furniture was pushed against the damask-hung walls and the rugs rolled back. The pianist struck a commanding chord on the piano, while her son wrestled the first note out of his accordion.

Up and down the shining parquet we raced. Strip the Willow, the Dashing White Sergeant, eightsome reels, foursome reels, sixteensome reels, the Duke of Perth, and Petronella – nobody dreamed of sitting out a single dance. One of my ancestresses had composed a strathspey that was known by the name of the castle, and this was always included in the evening's music. At midnight, the chauffeurs were summoned from their games of whist in the servants' hall, hot soup was handed around, and sheepskin coats were thrown over evening clothes. Missing girls emerged, bright-eyed, from unexpected corners, to be followed seconds later by self-conscious young men. Addresses were scribbled on starched shirt cuffs, and promises for future meetings exchanged. Half-frozen engines spluttered in the courtyard, car doors slammed, and red tail-lights vanished down the drive.

After that first hockey party, I went up to my bedroom in the tower too excited to sleep. It had been used as one of the changing-rooms for the girls; I opened the window to let out the warm, powder-scented air, and leaned on the sill, gazing into the darkness .... The winter night was utterly silent – no dog barked, no owl screeched in the frozen forests. Then suddenly, like a vast golden curtain, the aurora borealis swept along the northern horizon. For a moment, the lights hung motionless, then they wavered and changed to pink. It seemed that I heard a sharp sound, like the crack of a whip – could it have come from the sky, or could it have been that the shifting lights, recalling to my subconscious the chromatic cloaks of clowns, gave me the impression that I was the solitary spectator of some stupendous celestial circus, commanded by a spectral scarlet-coated ringmaster? But as the sound ... ricocheted away down the ice-fringed river, the lights in the sky changed to mauve and blue and then, shifting sideways, dissolved, to reappear a moment later in stripes of brightest silver. For several minutes, a hundred miles from the surface of the earth, the lights shifted, forming and reforming in columns and ribbons and draperies of ever-changing colours, and then, as suddenly as they had appeared, they vanished, and I was left rubbing my eyes, half dazed with sleep, wondering if the whole vision had been a dream.

In winter we also went ski-ing. Even the most watery sun would, when its rays were reflected by miles of unbroken snow, provide enough light to guide us as we searched the lofts for skis. These skis were long, heavy, and rigid – not mountain skis but trekking skis, made for traversing the flat wastes of the Arctic. At the ski runs, we strapped them onto our heavily-nailed winter boots and ... precipitated ourselves down the slopes. Nobody taught us how to turn or stop – we just plunged downhill until we either reached the bottom or fell.

But to reach our ski-runs, we had to journey again through darkness – the darkness of the pine-forests on the lower slopes of the hills. Little snow and still less light penetrated the bushy tops of the closely-planted trees, while underfoot the fallen pine-needles of past years, deepest green rotting into black, muffled the sound of our steps.

Soon after three o'clock in the afternoon, the sun began to sink and, as if to make up in the last half hour for its shortcomings during the day, nearly always produced a magnificent sunset. Hurrying home, we would see the western sky spattered with orange and vermilion, the undersides of the clouds ablaze with scarlet. Pink and grey and clearest lemon-yellow, the high cirrus filaments streamed in the upper reaches of the air. Sombre against the gold of the horizon, homing rooks cawed their way to their untidy nests in the village beeches. Ahead of us would stretch another seemingly interminable winter evening. Once the wooden shutters were unfolded over the windows, and the heavy curtains ... were drawn, we were, as far as entertainment was concerned, thrown back on our own resources.

~ *Christian Miller* ~

29th DECEMBER –
THE TAY BRIDGE DISASTER 1879

THE first Tay Railway Bridge was blown down in a storm while a train was passing over it with 78 passengers and crew, and the consequent loss of all lives (1879).

> It continued its way onwards, entered the high girders in the middle of the Bridge, and when just about to emerge from them at the north end, a fearful blast, with a noise like thunder, swept down the river. At that moment two intensely brilliant sheets of flame and showers of sparks were seen to rise from the high girders, evidently resulting from the friction of the ponderous ironwork as it crashed and tumbled into the river below from the horrible height of about 100 feet. Simultaneously with the disappearance of the sparks and flashes of light the train also disappeared; and before they had time to realise their fearful position, the whole of the 200 passengers were ushered into eternity.

> *~ Dundee Courier and Argus,*
> Monday 29th December, 1879 ~

[This extract illustrates how newspapers are prone to exaggeration – their estimate of 200 dead was way over the top – *eds*.]

VICTORIAN EDINBURGH DIARY –
CHRISTMAS

25th December 1879 – THURSDAY:

Christmas. At office at 10 o'clock. In the Statue Gallery in the forenoon. In the afternoon home and dug up the garden with a nice little spade I got from Black. Teen went off at 6.30 p.m. to see Miss Lawson's marriage while I kept the boy. She returned about 9.00 p.m., the boy meanwhile having behaved himself very well. The boy got a Christmas card addressed to him from Tib today.

28th December – SUNDAY:

Very stormy and windy today, especially towards nightfall and in the evening. Went out a turn about 12 o'clock for an hour. Home again. The bad weather prevented our getting out for a walk ....

29th December – MONDAY:

Teen up early washing. Read *The Scotsman* and learned that a train going towards Dundee had been last night about 7 o'clock hurled over the Tay Bridge by the force of the wind, the whole of the over arching girders in the centre of the bridge being carried bodily off so that not a vestige of the whole was visible. The number of passengers in the train, who of course all perished, was at first estimated at 300, but later in the day it was estimated at a much lower figure *viz.* 70. The talk has of course been of little else all day, the accident being almost unprecedented in the annals of earthly disasters. Not home in the middle of the day. Going about the town paying accounts for Sir James Fergusson. Bought *Man On Lescaut.* Read the preface to it by Jules Janin. Teen was very busy all day and I was a little cross in the evening keeping John. Miss Lawson called in the evening and brought a small piece of Bridescake for Mr Miller *etc.* Teen washed the curtains ....

~ *John Inglis* ~

THE CHRISTMAS GUIZARDS
(Gloucestershire Wassail)

~ Music collected by
Ralph Vaughan Williams ~

THE CHRISTMAS GUIZARDS
(Gloucestershire Wassail)

Het pint! Het pint! Oot ower the toun!
Oor breid it is white an oor yill it is broun.
Oor coggie is made o the reid rowan tree.
Wi a stoup o guid swats we'll drink tae thee.

Sae hale be tae auld Prince an tae his richt cheek,
Pray God send oor maister a fine daud o beef,
An a fine daud o beef that may we aa see;
Wi a stoup o guid swats we'll drink tae thee.

An hale be tae Maggie an tae her richt foot,
Pray God send the maister a swack Christmas pudd;
An a swack Christmas pudd that may we aa see;
Wi a stoup o guid swats we'll drink tae thee.

An hale be tae Daisy an tae her left ear,
Pray God send the maister a happy New Year,
An a happy New Year as e'er he did see;
Wi a cog o guid swats we'll drink tae thee.

Come landlord, come fill us a stoup o the best,
Then we'll hope that yer sowl in haiven may rest;
But gin an ye draw us a pint o the sma
Then doun we'll coup landlord, stoup an aa!

Then here's tae the quine in the lilywhite sark
Wha link'd tae the door in spite o the dark,
Wha link'd tae the door an pu'd back the pin
For tae let thae canty guizards come in.

~ Traditional; owerset by Marjory Greig ~

ISLAND YULE

URING the solstice, the sun seemed to stand still. The Norsemen kept the twelve days from December 22 as the festival of Jul, and all work involving a circular action ceased. The flail was not used, nor the rotating quern stones. Cartwheels, spindles, all were still. In the remote northern isles, occupied for centuries by the people of western Norway, Yule has always been a special time.

At the turn of the century in North Ronaldsay, the low stone houses were outwardly silent and dark in the biting wind, but inside there was noise and bustle. The rooms had all been cleaned and scrubbed, and veronica decorated the mantelpiece with its white wally dugs and tea tins. Crisp oatcakes had been baked on the iron yetling, or girdle, and bere bannocks big as soup plates, cooled on a wire tray.

A pig had been killed, when the moon was waxing, and there was pork to fry. There was mutton from the Yule sheep specially chosen at the Yule Pund, when all the men went to the shore to catch a fat healthy sheep for the family. Mealy puddings were made from the oatmeal ground in the island mill, and stored in the wooden girnel. A woman's reputation depended on the bere bannocks, mutton, and mealy puddings provided for neighbours who came to bring in the New Year.

Outside in the barn and brewhouse the men had been brewing ale. Malt was made from bere, the primitive form of barley still grown on the island. The bere was threshed and dressed, steeped in water, dried, spread out on a stone floor and turned. It was dried in the kiln, winnowed, cleaned and crushed. Then the malt was ready. Some women were famous for brewing good ale. There were ancient superstitions connected with this particular Yule brewing, but by the turn of the century they had disappeared. In Scandinavia crossed sickles were fixed above the brewhouse door, and a silver coin or ring was placed in the brewing vessel. During the fermentation process, extreme care was necessary, and the process had to be helped by loud yells and singing.

The malt was put in a big wooden vat and covered with boiling water for two hours, then the wort was drained off. This liquid was boiled for two and a half hours, then strained and cooled. A little was mixed with yeast, to start it barming. The ale was finally bottled and left.

Yule was the season when relatives at distant crofts were visited. A small girl at that time was bathed in the wooden washtub, her long hair washed and dried at the fire, and tied up in long strips of cotton rags the night before. Her petticoat was white with a broderie anglaise edging, over which she wore a pink woollen crocheted underskirt; her chemise was hand sewn with the neatest of stitches. She wore long black knitted stockings, a thick skirt of navy serge, and a white long sleeved blouse, with pearl buttons and a sailor collar.

Horses were not usually harnessed at night, and the lantern was lit for a journey on foot, or visits were made in bright moonlight. In the firelit kitchen it was warm and bright, in the soft glow of the oil lamp hanging from the ceiling. It was exciting to sit at the table set with the wedding china, polished spoons, fruit cake, and 'cakey shortbread' from the Mainland, brought by the steamer. There was a decoration of coloured icing, holly and robins, with 'Merry Christmas' or 'Happy New Year'. On the shelf of the dresser were the Christmas plates, with their seasonal messages. Christmas cards were different then, much smaller, and often delicately coloured.

At a time when Christmas was celebrated less than Hogmanay, it was interesting to hear that this particular child, Sarah, hung up her stocking on the brass rod above the black kitchen range every Christmas Eve, and got a doll, an orange and an apple, a shilling, and sweeties. The doll was brought back every year by her father from the Lammas Fair, and hidden. My father-in-law and his brother, in their mid-eighties, told me about their Christmasses in 1908-9. On Christmas Eve they took off their little woollen socks, and each hung one on the brass rod. In the morning there was a small toy, like a tiny set of toy scales, and an orange or a poke of pandrops or conversation lozenges.

Every year the laird's wife at Holland House had a Christmas party for all the island children, with a real tree. Each child was given a slip of paper with a number on it, and each got a present, a sewing set, or a tiny rigged sailing ship.

Hogmanay was the most important day, with its own customs. Every woman had to make sure all the washing was done, so that there were no dirty clothes in the house for the New Year. The floor was swept inwards towards the fire, so that luck wasn't swept out of the house. There were football matches on the links, the young people walked to the lighthouse, and there was a dance. The men of the township met on the evening of Hogmanay, and visited each house in turn, where they were given mutton, bere bannocks, oatcakes, cheese, and as much ale as they could drink. Woe betide the woman who was not free handed with her hospitality. Sometimes the ale was heated on the fire with sugar and poured steaming into spongeware ale cans, which I use for plants, and which are fashionable now. Old ballads were sung, like 'The Bride's Lament', 'The Braes of Balquhidder' and 'The Ship That Never Returned'. Tales from long ago were retold, who was sib to whom, and other details of genealogy, and there was dancing, eating and drinking until dawn had come again.

The celebrations went on for several days, since some households stuck to the Old Calendar in any case, for Yule was a bright light in the darkness of winter, something to look forward to, and to remember afterwards.

~ Christine Muir ~

NEW YEAR COMES IN

New Year comes in
an every day
da light draas oot
bi smaa's:
da dark gies in,
as, nightly night,
later da huemin
faas.
Last year's lambs
we hed set in
ta get dem learned
ta aet,
comes tae da box,
an rins an shivs,
ta see what dey
can get.
Da ram set in,
wattered an fed,
an daated laek
a loard,
gets aa da best
athin his mooth
his crofter can
afford.
Da yowes at lies
aboot da knowes,
blyde o da bit
o lee,
gets sometin too
ta keep dir herts,
an da lambs at sune
ta be.
An doon below
ati da root,
da peerie flooers
stirs,
blyde o da dark
ta shalter dem

oot o da winter's
birss.
Some folk never
saw dis year;
some's waitin
ta come in;
some finished wi
da rule o Time,
some ready
ta begin.
An dir a lock mair
gaen on
at's nedder heard
nor seen,
dey'll be a power
o spaekin o,
afore da next
Newe'r E'en!

~ Stella Sutherland ~

31st DECEMBER – HOGMANAY

HOGMANAY; Gaelic *Oidhche Chaluinne*:
From the French dialect *hoguiané*, French *agguillanneuf*, a song sung by children going from door to door for New Year gifts.

On FIRST-FOOTING:
'The first-fit generally carries with him a hot beverage, made of ale, spirits, eggs, cream, sugar, and biscuit, with some slices of curran bun to be eaten along with it, or perhaps some bread and cheese.'

~ *E Picken* from *Dictionary of the Scottish Language, 1818* ~

THE LAST NIGHT OF THE YEAR

OF all the Red Letter Days in the Scots calendar, Hogmanay, the last night of the year, is perhaps the most beloved. Hearts are opened, warm friendship and kindly deeds abound. It is supposed to have had its origin in the flitting of the Little People, the expulsion of all bad things and the moving in of a new set of fairies with a load of Good Luck.

The traditional First Foot, the first dark man to cross the threshold, brought gifts representing Plenty in fuel, food, and drink. In the old days he carried in his pocket his personal First Footing cup, in shape like a whisky glass in copper or brass. The stem unscrewed and fitted into the reversed cup when not in use ... unhygienic, but very handy when offering or receiving a dram. First Footing doubtless took place in the Glen in my childhood, with visiting neighbours bearing gifts of shortbread and black bun, and drams continually refilling First Footing cups, but we saw none of that at the Manse.

In Ballater, in the early 1890s and possibly later, the chief excitement on Hogmanay night was the arrival of the village lads with blackened faces and wearing weird costumes, who called at every house to perform a traditional play, which had among its characters Galashan with his sword and pistol, Sir William Wallace, and good old Doctor Broon, 'the best auld doctor in the toon'. In countless forms this play is known all over the British Isles and is of great antiquity.

At the Manse Ellie and I arrayed ourselves in our notion of fancy dress and put on home-made masks, our so-called 'false faces'. First, we went to the study door to serenade my father, and then to carol to my mother, amid explosive giggles, the old rhyme she had taught us ....

Rise up, good wife, and shake your feathers,
Don't think that we are beggars,
We are children come to play,
Rise up and give's our Hogmanay!
Up sticks! Down stools!
Don't think that we are fools,
We are children come to play,
Rise up and give's our Hogmanay!

Our Hogmanay consisted of an apple, sweet biscuits, cake and sweeties.

~ Amy Stewart Fraser ~

HOGMANAY SONG

~ Music by Margaret Sinclair ~

HOGMANAY SONG

Get up Guidwife, and binna swear,
And deal your breid tae them that's here;
For the time will come when we'll be deid –
And ye'll neither need ale nor breid.

CHORUS:
Hogmanay, Trollolay.
Give us of your white breid and none of your grey.

My shoon are made of hoary hide,
Behind the door I downa bide;
My tongue is sair, I daurna sing –
I fear I will get little thing.

CHORUS:
Hogmanay, Trollolay *etc.*

Rise up Guidwife, and shak your feathers,
And dinna think that we are beggars.
We are but bairnies come to play,
Rise up and gie's our Hogmanay.

CHORUS:
Hogmanay, Trollolay *etc.*

Up sticks! Down stools!
Dinna think that we are fools.
We are but bairnies come to play,
Rise up and gie's our Hogmanay.

CHORUS:
Hogmanay, Trollolay.
Give us of your white breid and none of your grey.

~ Words: *Traditional* ~

HOGMANAY AT ABBOTSFORD

THE whole of the ancient ceremonial of the *Daft Days*, as they are called in Scotland, obtained respect at Abbotsford. Scott said it was *uncanny* not to welcome the new year in the midst of his family and a few old friends, with the immemorial libation of a *het pint*; but of all the consecrated ceremonies of the time, none gave him such delight as the visit which he received as *Laird* from all the children on his estate, on the last morning of every December – when, in the words of an obscure poet often quoted by him,

> 'The cottage bairns sing blythe and gay,
> At the ha' door for Hogmanay.'

~ John Gibson Lockhart ~

THE Scottish labourer is in his natural state perhaps one of the best, most intelligent and kind-hearted of human beings; and in truth I have limited my other habits of expense very much since I fell into the habit of employing mine honest people. I wish you could have seen about a hundred children, being almost entirely supported by their fathers' or brothers' labour, come down yesterday to dance to the pipes, and get a piece of cake and bannock, and pence-a-piece in honour of *hogmanay*. I declare to you, my dear friend, that when I thought the poor fellows who kept those children so neat, and well taught, and well-behaved, were slaving the whole day for eighteen-pence, or twenty-pence at the most, I was ashamed of their gratitude ....

~ Sir Walter Scott ~

HET PINT

Grate a nutmeg into two quarts of mild ale and bring it to the point of boiling. Mix a little cold ale with sugar necessary to sweeten this and add three eggs well beaten. Gradually mix the hot ale with the eggs, taking care that they do not curdle. Put in half a pint of whisky and bring once more nearly to boiling point. Then briskly pour it from one vessel to another till it becomes smooth and bright.

~ Meg Dods's recipe ~

BLACK BUN
(A Festive Cake at Hogmanay)

Thou tuck-shop king! Joy of our gourmand youth!
    What days thou mark'st, and what blood-curdling nights!
Nights full of shapeless things, hideous, uncouth;
    Imp follows ghoul, ghoul follows jinn, pell mell;
Fierce raisin-devils and gay currant-sprites
    Hold lightsome leap-frog in a pastry hell.

~ Augustus Bejant, 'Invocation to Black Bun'
from the Glasgow University Magazine ~

1 lb flour	$\frac{1}{2}$ oz ground cloves or cinnamon
2 lbs currants	$\frac{1}{2}$ oz ground ginger
2 lbs Valencia raisins	1 teaspoonful Jamaica pepper
$\frac{1}{2}$ lb almonds	$\frac{1}{2}$ teaspoonful black pepper
$\frac{1}{2}$ lb mixed candied peel	small teaspoonful bicarbonate of soda
4 oz sugar	buttermilk or egg to moisten
1-2 tablespoonfuls brandy	

CRUST: 1 lb flour, $\frac{1}{2}$ lb butter, water

Wash and dry the currants. Stone the raisins. Blanch and chop the almonds. Chop the peel. Sift the flour into a basin, and add the sugar, spices, and prepared fruits. If buttermilk is used, stir the soda into it before moistening the cake; if egg, add the soda with the dry ingredients. Add the brandy first so that the mixture should not become wet. It should be merely moist.

Make a paste by rubbing the butter into the flour and adding just enough water to make a stiff dough, and roll out thinly. Grease a large cake-tin and line it evenly with the paste, retaining enough to cover the top. Trim the edges, put the mixture in, flatten the surface, moisten the edges of the paste with cold water, put on the lid of the pastry, and make all secure and neat. With a skewer make four holes right down to the bottom of the cake; then prick all over with a fork, brush with beaten egg, and bake in a moderate oven for about four hours.

This cake should be made several weeks, or even months, before it is to be used, so that it may mature and mellow.

Black Bun always appears on Hogmanay.

~ Recipe by F Marian McNeill ~

THE NEW YEAR HIMSELF

'AT Reachfar,' I said, 'this thirty-first of December Day was called Hogmanay.' 'Hogmanay,' Helga repeated, 'and what did George and Tom and Janet do on Hogmanay?'

'They fed all the indoor animals as usual,' I told her, 'and went round the moor and the hill to see that the sheep were all right, but after that it was a holiday and the three of them would get into Tom's bed and do a bit of reading or talking until dinnertime. It was usually snowy or frosty or sleety on Hogmanay, very wintry in some way, you know, but it was warm in Tom's bed .... So they would read until dinnertime and after that the Reachfar kitchen would become very busy for there would be a party that night. Reachfar was one of the houses where the people of the district gathered to bring the New Year in, so there was a big dumpling to be made and fresh scones and oatcakes to be baked and Tom and George and Janet had a special job to do. They had to dig up the kebbuck.'

'What was the kebbuck?'

'It was a cheese that Herself had made, a cheese about this much round' – I held my hands about two feet apart – 'and about this much high' – I indicated about a foot of height – '*and* very heavy. George, Tom and Janet had buried it in a corner of the garden at Hallowe'en ....'

'Why did they bury the kebbuck?'

'Cheese tastes better if you keep it for a time before you eat it .... At Hallowe'en it was wrapped in white muslin, then layers and layers of paper, then sacking and then it was buried in this hole in the garden, and on Hogmanay Tom and George and Janet dug it up, took all the sacking and paper off, carried it into the house and put it on top of the meal barrel in the corner of the kitchen. For Janet ... the kebbuck was not just a cheese. For her, it was part of the magic of the New Year.'

'And then all the people came and they had the party?'

'Yes. John the Smith and his sons would come and the men from Poyntdale and Dinchory and Danny the Beeman would bring his fiddle and Janet would dance the Highland Fling to his music. And more and more people would come and the dumpling would be eaten and Herself would cut the kebbuck with her big knife and it would begin to disappear too.

'One very dark, stormy Hogmanay, two strangers arrived at Reachfar. They were tinkers, sort of travelling gypsies. Tinkers were always given shelter and food at Reachfar, but usually they were put into one of the out-buildings. They lived out of doors most of the time, you see, and did not wash very much and Herself did not like to have them in the house; but on this Hogmanay she brought them in and put them into the Wee Room, as it was called, a little room under the stairs that had a broken-down old bed in it and a few boxes and odds and ends. Janet helped to carry some food to them. They were a young woman and a young man, very ragged and cold .... Janet invited the tinkers to come to the party in the kitchen, but they didn't want to and Herself said not to bother them, so Janet left them alone ....

'This was the first time she had ever been allowed to stay up till midnight to see the New Year come in. She had a sort of silly idea that, at midnight, the New Year would come walking in through the door like a visitor, but at the same time she knew that it was something that would start just after the clock on the mantel struck twelve. As midnight came near, the party became quieter. The dancing and the music stopped and everybody began to watch the hands of the clock. Janet knew the habits of that clock so she was the first to know that the New Year had nearly come for the clock went "Ip-it-see!", the little noise that it made before it went "Ting, ting, ting – " as it struck the hour.

'It began to strike now and everybody stood up and Janet suddenly realised that her grandmother was not in the kitchen. This scared Janet, for Herself was always there when anything important happened at Reachfar; but just as the clock finished striking the twelfth ring, Herself came in and she was carrying a little white bundle. It was a baby boy that had just been born to the tinker woman in the Wee Room. Herself looked down at Janet and said: "This is the New Year himself, Janet. You hold him now for a minute and then we'll take him back to his mother." Janet held the baby very carefully and felt that her grandmother, who was so wise that she knew everything, had known of her idea that the New Year would come in like a visitor. Then Janet carried the baby back to his mother and father in the Wee Room.'

'And did the tinker people and their baby stay at Reachfar?' Helga asked.

'No. When Janet came downstairs the next morning, they were gone. The New Year was gone too. It was just another day in another year .... The magic feeling was gone.'

'And the kebbuck?'

'Nothing was left of it except some crumbs and some rind on top of the meal barrel. The big white sow had them as a special treat ....

There was another thing that happened at Reachfar on Hogmanay,' I said .... 'Danny the Beeman used to go out of the house just before midnight and come in again when the clock had finished striking. He was called the First Foot, the first person to come into the house in the New Year. It was always Danny because he was very dark. He had black hair, very dark eyes and brown skin, and dark First Foots were supposed to bring good luck. That night I told you about, Danny came in just after Herself and the tinker baby. He had a cake of shortbread and a bottle of whisky in one hand and this meant that he hoped that the house would have plenty to eat and drink for the rest of the year. In the other hand he had a log of wood which he put on the fire. This meant that he hoped that the house would be warm for the rest of the year. And that year of the baby, he tied a silver sixpence into the corner of the bit of blanket that wrapped the baby, which meant that he hoped the baby would be rich one day.'

~ Jane Duncan ~

OPEN THE DOOR

Open the door for the auld year,
It is the pairtin-time:
Open the door for the new year
And lat the bairn win hame.

Bundle your winter'd joy and grief
On the back o' the year that's düne:
Open your hert for the new life
And lat the bairn come in.

~ William Soutar ~

1880 COMES IN

31st December

JOHN came down at 7.30 in the morning with the groceries. In the evening I was back at the office about coupons to be sent to London. Brought down the Cash Book and List and wraught at them at home. We stayed up till after midnight. Mr and Mrs Dow came in and were our 'first foot'. Went and paid my tailor's bill and got the pamphlet 'Plundering and Blundering'.

1st January, 1880

At office by about 10 a.m. Home again at 2.15. Jamie Mitchell in. Back to office again at 3.45 p.m. At G.P.O. about 5.00. Saw Herbert McLaren and his little boy going to the soiree in the Music Hall. He is rather hard up it appears and his wife is badly. He was almost begging. Home about 5.30. Teen very tired and done out today. Tea a little before 7.00. Then we went out and walked the boy up and down the street to give him the fresh air. Very windy but very fine. Then came in and adjourned to the room, where the boy was quite pleased with the change. Then John Inglis called and stayed nearly an hour. He had been at Reid Terrace at tea.

~ John Inglis ~

REDDING-UP FOR NEW YEAR

IF we didn't decorate the house for Christmas, we had a positive orgy of cleaning for Hogmanay. Grannie and I shone the steels on the range, the brass covers on the dresser, and the brass gas-bracket, door-knob and letter-box till they sparkled like gold. The flues were cleaned. The floor polished. My mother washed all the furniture in the room with vinegar water, polished the tiles on the fireplace till they looked like amber, and rubbed the polished mantelpiece … to a gleaming satin.

The 'room' was the best room in the house, and it was in fact the only room, apart from the kitchen, where we ate, and lived, and where Grannie and I slept, and we were well disciplined to accept that in the 'room' we must not romp or play …. We shared our mother's anxiety that it should be kept nice for 'folk coming' and for special occasions, and the most splendid of all occasions was Hogmanay. This was the only time food was brought into the room. At other times, nobody would have dared risk dropping food or drink on our best things. But at Hogmanay – ah! that was different.

A table was set near the window, spread with our best white cloth, lace-trimmed, and on it was laid the best china. Plates were laden with Genoa cake (my mother's favourite), cherry cake, Dundee cake, a round cake of shortbread and shortbread fingers. There was a wee bit of black bun for those who liked it, but it was only the very oldest members of the company who seemed to enjoy nibbling it. We children never touched it. There was a tray with bottles of port, sherry and ginger wines. However poor the tenement people were, they could always manage a few bottles for Hogmanay. Glasses sat on another tray. On the sideboard the best crystal bowl was filled with oranges and tangerines for the Hogmanay visitors, and we gazed at them enviously, but would never have dreamt of touching them ….

When it grew dark my mother put a match to the fire in the grate, and soon the blaze was reflecting itself in the amber tiles, and everything was poised, in lovely cleanliness, waiting for the magic hour of midnight when the New Year would be ushered in.

We children were in our pyjamas by this time, and the minute the bells were announcing midnight, we were given a wee sip of home-made ginger wine and a bit of shortbread, then whisked off to bed in the kitchen. We would lie listening for the first-foots arriving, and we'd fall asleep to the sound of conversation and doors opening and shutting, and shouts of 'Happy New Year, an' mony o' them'. Occasionally a voice could be heard in the lobby, asking, 'Are the weans in their beds? Och here's something for their pocket. Gi'e it to them in the morning', and sleepily we would wonder if it would be a threepenny bit or a sixpence that we'd have for our darkie bank when we wakened up.

~ Molly Weir ~

THE MIDWINTER MUSIC –
NEW YEAR

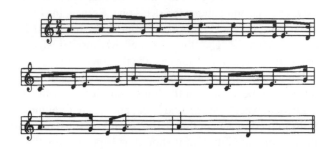

YULE is the festival of innocence. New Year, seven days later, is the festival of experience, that measures time and hopes and dreads everything.

The young men gather, a group of a dozen or more singers, on the last night of the year. Among them is the Fool, whom they call the 'kairyin horse', the beast of burden, the scapegoat. A curse and a blessing are on him; he is liable to be roughly handled by the choir of young men, kicked and thrown about, whenever the fancy takes them; but when it comes to the distribution of food and drink he is given a larger share than the others, and this too as the old year dies becomes a further occasion for recrimination and insult.

The family round the peat fire hear a distant singing on the road, in the darkness of the last night of the year ....

The crofter takes the door off the latch. The croft lamp throws a weak waver of light outside. The singers stand at the edge of it, a glitter of eyes. They chant.

> This night is guid New'ar ev'n's night
> *We're a' Saint Mary's men*
> An' we've come here tae crave wur right
> *Fore wur Lady.*

> The morn it is guid New'ar Day
> *We're a' Saint Mary's men*
> An' we've come here tae sport and play
> *Fore wur Lady.*

Neighbours are calling with good wishes to neighbour. Yet the refrain insists that the neighbourliness is not entirely secular. The Virgin Mary, Our Lady, Queen of Heaven, is also invited to be present. (We can assume the sacred chorus for the rest of the song.) Secular and holy link hands in the dance.

A light threatening tone enters; but however the mood changes – and the song is full of twists and turns – the festive note is constant.

> An' if we get no' what we seek
> We'll tak the head of your Yule Sheep.

The blessing is resumed, is broadened to include all the creatures of stable and byre and barnyard. The crofter opens the door a little further. A cow lows in the byre, pigs shift and grunt in the stye. The women and children listen beside the fire. A kirn of ale seethes in a dark corner. The table is loaded with cheese, boiled fowls, bannocks, slices of mutton. The song runs on through the sluice of the open door, merry as a winter burn in spate.

> May a' your kye be weel tae calf
> An' every ane hae a queyo calf
>
> May a' your mares be weel tae foal
> An' every ane hae a mare foal
>
> May a' your yowes be weel tae lamb
> An' every ane hae a yowe an' a ram
>
> May a' your geese be weel tae t'rive
> An' every ane hae three times five
>
> May a' your hens rin in a reel
> An' every ane twal' at her heel.

At this point the man of the house opens his door wide, so that he stands framed in the lamplight, and the singers can see the compact excited family round the fire; and the grandmother and the children can see the circle of ghosts with red merry mouths in the frosty darkness outside.

> Whaur is the guidman o' this hoose?
> Whaur is he, that man?
>
> An' why is he no' as before
> At the opening o' the door?

Whaur is the guidwife o' this hoose?
Whaur is she, that dame?

An' why is she no' as before
Wi' her full cog under faim?

Whaur is the servant lass o' this hoose?
Whaur is she, that lass?

And why is she no' as afore
In sweepin' oot the asse?

Whaur is the servant man o' this hoose?
Whaur is he, that lad?

And why is he no as afore
Oot dellin' wi' a spade?

This night is guid New'ar ev'n's night
An' we've come here tae claim wur right.

Now the singers have a full view of the loaded table inside. All is well with this farm after all, thank God. Let the crofter and his wife do their duty then. The choir is cold and hungry. If these bearers of luck and blessing receive their due, good fortune will bide in this house in the year to come. The wheel turns; the *de profundis* chant becomes suddenly a fantasy of wealth and abundance. They will be richer than the laird himself. They will have wide acres and trading ships on the sea. The flattery merges into a ritual boasting that includes the whole community of the island in wished-for prosperity and affluence – all except the mean wife where they last visited; what the singers will do to her they hint at darkly and lewdly.

The last hoose that we were at
'Twas there we got but ae bere cake.

The jade that baked it sae thin
Merry an' wanton may she rin.

We hae wur ships sailan the sea
An mighty men o lands are we.

> We hae wur stacks stanein'
> And we hae wur ploos gangin'.
>
> We hae wur fat gilts in the stye
> A few tae sell an nane tae buy.

Yes, all this wealth would be theirs in actual fact, but for one dreadful burden that they must bear all the days of their life; and with one accord they turn on the clown of the party, the 'kairyin horse', whose duty it is to hump round the surplus food and drink that has been given them in the various crofts, and they kick him and buffet him in mock earnest; for the singers and the crofter their host would indeed be rich farmers and traders were they not kept in poverty by the inordinate appetites of their beast to whom they have been so good. The Fool symbolises now prodigality, wastefulness, gluttony, stupidity, all that drags a man and his estate into penury, all the taxes and stipends and feus and excise duties and rents that keep him bound for ever to the plough and the grindstone.

> Here we hae wur kairyin horse
> An' muckle vengence fa' his corse
>
> For he wad eat mair meat
> Or a' that we can gaither an get
>
> An' he wad drink mair drink
> Or a' that we can swither or swink

With a wild mixture of threatening, cajolery, joy, impudence the song ends. The door is flung wide. Faces pinched with the cold crowd about the blazing peat-fire and festive board. The meal is eaten standing. It is a reward for all the labour of the past year that has been done in the parish, a gathering of strength for the work of the year to come, a ritual feast rounded with song and dancing and prayer.

> Be ye maids or be ye nane
> Ye's a' be kissed or we gang hame
>
> Guidwife, just lift your ambry lid
> An' fetch the busslins an' the redd
>
> An' the three-lugged cog that's standing fu'
> Fetch it here tae weet wur mou'

This is the best that we can tak'
An' we will drink till wur lugs crack.

This is the sevent' night o Yule
We're a' Saint Mary's men
An' b' me saul I think it'll fail
Fore wur Lady.

~ *George Mackay Brown* ~

~ Music: *Traditional* ~

HOGMANAY 1963

Husky bells on the television swing out the old
year, wrung with doubts and shrugged uncertainties
new-every-morning; somehow, ours no longer,
downed by the stroke of twelve, turned history's.

There's a shift of foot by responsibility:
the pursed accountant rounds on the farmer's wife
beneath the mistletoe; some matron's chiffoned breasts
image surrender to a salesman's strife;

the young forget The Bomb; their elders' dreams
of dividends, like bubbles in a glass,
evaporate. Finalities retreat
as hopeful shifts of newer purpose mass,

only to be dissolved by sleep, or sluggish dregs
of resolutioned hangovers. Whatever fear
crouches beneath our breathing, licks us awake
to difference we neither see nor hear;

nor smell, like fields of rain. Though nothing mends,
it is good that make-do time grants such respites –
semblances of completeness, endings without ends –
where each of us, according to our lights

safe in our warm enclosure of experience,
forgets the cold outside; the invisible, slow
erosion of what seemed to mean much more,
brushed-at by mists of promises tears ago.

~ *Maurice Lindsay* ~

THE AULD YEAR

CHORUS:
Ding! ding! Bells o the Barony:
Ding! ding! Deeve us an' a'.
Ding! ding! Hogmanay harmony,
Naebody greets for the year that's awa'

Auld year, we hoped to dae weel in the days o' ye:
Muckle ye promised but little cam' true.
Noo the bells ring, but it's no for the praise o' ye
Cast the auld bauchles, an' hansel the new.

CHORUS: Ding! ding! Bells o the Barony, *etc.*

Auld year, your secrets are nae mair a mystery;
Hoo ye begunkit us brawly ye ken.
Ilka new year is a clean page in history:
Turn ower the leaf, an' tak' tent wi' your pen.

CHORUS: Ding! ding! Bells o the Barony, *etc.*

~ Music by *Margaret Sinclair; words by W D Cocker* ~

NEW YEAR'S EVE

THE little parlour of the old people's modest abode at Rothesay was a picture of hospitality and kindness personified. The Robinson family had just arrived from Glasgow, and after a chilly, though not unpleasant journey were enjoying the comforts of the tea-table, Macgregor's appetite being, as usual, remarkably keen, especially for the luxuries ....

'Mind and leave room fur yer supper, laddie,' Mr Purdie said.

'Are we gaun to get supper furbye?' exclaimed the boy in gratified surprise.

'Na, na,' said Lizzie. 'Yer Grandpaw's jist jokin'. Ye maun gang early to yer bed the nicht, an' ha'e a fine day ootbye the morn – if it's no ower cald or wat.'

'I dinna want to gang to ma bed early, Maw. I want to bring in the New Year.'

'Oh, ye're ower wee to sit up that late, dearie.'

'I'm no, Maw! Wullie Thomson's maw is gaun to let him sit up, an' he's faur wee-er nor me.'

His mother shook her head. 'I canna help whit Mistress Thomson lets Wullie dae. Maybe that's whit maks him peely-wally – sittin' up late isna guid fur laddies ....'

Lizzie was at a loss, and her husband said boldly: 'Let Macgreegor bring in the New Year, wumman.'

'An let him hae his supper like the rest o us,' added Mr Purdie.

'Jist that,' said Mrs Purdie, beaming across the table.

Mrs Robinson laughed ruefully ... 'I dinna believe in late suppers for weans, an' I doot Macgreegor'll be needin' to get ile i' the mornin'.'

'I'll tak the ile, Maw,' said Macgregor so eagerly that everybody laughed.

Presently the party rose from the table and gathered round the fire, where the elders sat chatting for an hour, at the end of which Mrs Purdie set about clearing the tea things ....

'Are ye wearyin', Macgreegor?' asked Mr Purdie.

Macgregor replied, 'Dae a recite, Grandpaw.'

'Haud yer tongue, Macgreegor,' said John gently.

But Mr Purdie genially replied, 'An' whit wad ye like me to recite ma mannie?'

'Dae yin aboot folk gettin' kilt. Dae yon yin aboot the man that drooned the ither man an' then got nabbit by the ghost. Thon's an awfu' nice yin!' he added with a slight shudder.

'Na, na. That's no a story fur Hogmanay, laddie.'

'Aw ay, Granpaw,' said Macgregor, leaving his perch, and standing persuasively at Mr Purdie's knee. 'An' then dae the yin aboot the skeletin in the boax ....'

Mr Purdie smilingly shook his head, but was eventually persuaded to get out his old recitation book ....

Ere long Mrs Purdie and Lizzie, who had both been very busy in the kitchen, appeared, and proceeded to lay the table for supper.

Macgregor kept silence awhile, but at last, Lizzie being alone, out burst the question: 'Whit are we to get, Maw?'

His mother bit her lip and pretended not to hear him.

'Maw, whit's that nice smell?' he whispered.

'It'll be naethin' fur you, if ye dinna haud yer tongue,' she replied in a severe undertone.

He held his peace for a couple of minutes. Then, in a tone of the tenderest inquiry: 'Is't a pie, Maw?'

Lizzie replied with a look of solemn warning.

'Am I to get leemonade, Maw?'

'John!' she cried desperately. 'Can ye no gie Macgreegor something to keep him quate?'

'He's no makin' a noise, is he?' said John, who had dropped into a chat with his father-in-law. 'What is't ye're wantin, ma laddie?'

'I was jist speirin whit we wis gaun to get to ....'

Just then ... old Mrs Purdie entered smiling. 'Are ye a' ready fur yer suppers?'

'Ay!' replied Macgregor so promptly that the assents of the others were mere echoes.

'Weel, ma dearie,' said his grandmother, 'come awa' wi' me an' help to cairry the plates.'

He followed her to the kitchen, and there cried in triumph: 'I kent it wis a pie!'

'Aw, Macgreegor,' sighed his mother reproachfully.

A few minutes later there was not a cheerier little year-end party in Scotland ....

Grandfather Purdie laughed to his spouse across the table, as he flourished a large knife and fork. 'This'll no' be yer first Hogmanay pie, auld wife!' he cried.

She smiled. 'Ask a blessin', auld man,' she said softly.

'Dod, I near furgot!' he muttered apologetically, laying down the knife and fork; and, resting his right elbow on the table, he covered his eyes with his wrinkled hand ....

'Macgreegor gets helpit first fur bein' the youngest,' he said presently ....

It was a plenteous repast, seasoned throughout with benevolence and merriment. Mr Purdie told stories and chuckled; Mrs Purdie listened and beamed; John laughed and winked pleasantly at his wife; and Lizzie, having somehow relaxed her watchfulness over her son, enjoyed herself more than she usually did in company ....

The feast ended as happily as it began, and once more there was a gathering by the hearth, to while away the two hours that remained to the Old Year.

But now Macgregor was content to sit on the hassock while his grandfather gave one more reading .... And ere long the elders paused in their grown-up chat, and nodded, smiling, to the hearthrug, where the boy, having slipped from the hassock, lay sound asleep.

'Puir daurlin',' said his grandmother gently.

'He'll be wearit wi' the journey, nae doot,' said Mr Purdie ....

'John,' Lizzie said, 'wud ye no' pit him ower on the sofa?'

'Deed, ay,' replied John, and Macgregor, without protest, allowed himself to be carried to the temporary couch.

The old couple and the young talked, and talked, and talked ... of days gone by and of days to come. Now and then there fell a silence, and they would glance separately at the sleeper, and back to one another, smiling gently ....

'Mercy me!' cried Lizzie, pointing suddenly, 'It's twal' o'clock!'

The long hand of the old clock in the corner was only a minute from the hour.

'I maun wauken Macgreegor,' said John. 'He wud be sair disappintit if – '

'Ay; he maun hear the 'oor strikin',' said Mr Purdie, starting up. 'Haste ye, an' wauken him, John.'

But the boy was sleeping very sound.

'Macgreegor, Macgreegor, the New Year's comin' in!'

Macgregor grunted drowsily ....

Sounds rose in the street, and a voice bawled: 'A guid New Year to yin an' a'!'

'Whit a peety! He'll be ower late,' sighed Mrs Purdie ....

The jovial sounds from the street increased. A church clock boomed midnight.

'It's ower late,' sighed Mrs Purdie, John, and Lizzie as Macgregor at last sat up, blinking.

'Is't the New Year?' he asked.

'Ay, but – but …. '

A chuckle came from Grandfather Purdie. 'Na, it's no' ower late. It wants near a meenit to twal'.' And he pointed to the face of the old clock in front of which he was standing.

Macgregor rubbed his eyes and gazed.

'Listen,' said Mr Purdie. 'D'ye hear the Auld Year tickin' awa'? …. Noo, it's jist gaun to strike!' ….

'A guid New Year!' cried everybody to everybody else, and much handshaking ensued.

'Did ye like bringin' in the New Year, ma mannie?' inquired the old man a little later.

Macgregor, now fairly wide awake, replied: 'Ay, fine! But did the New Year come oot the nock, Granpaw?'

'Eh?'

'Whit wey is the wee door o' the nock open, Granpaw?'

Mr Purdie stared helplessly. 'I thocht I had shut it,' he muttered feebly.

'Whit wey?' began the boy again.

'Macgreegor, come to your bed, dearie,' Lizzie interrupted.

'But whit wey – '

'No' anither word! Ye maun ha'e a guid sleep noo, and be ready fur yer presents in the mornin'.' And she led him away.

'I wis near catched that time,' said Grandfather Purdie to himself. 'I wudna ha'e liket onybody to ha'e seen me haudin' the pendulum.' Mrs Purdie and John were talking together by the fire, and he went over to the clock and cautiously closed the door.

'Ay, ay, John,' Mrs Purdie was saying, a little sadly, as he joined them, 'Anither year bye! Time waits on nane o' us.'

John shook his head solemnly, but as the old woman continued gazing into the failing fire, he turned and winked sympathetically to his father-in-law.

~ J J Bell ~

GOD BE HERE

God be here, God be there,
We wiss ye aa a canty year;
God without, God within.
Lat the Auld Year oot
An the New Year in.

~ Traditional; owerset by *Marjory Greig ~*

AN ORMIDALE STEAK PIE
FOR HOGMANAY

1 $\frac{1}{4}$ lbs beef steak	1 teaspoonful Worcester sauce
$\frac{1}{4}$ lb kidney	1 teaspoonful tomato sauce
1 onion (optional)	1 teaspoonful vinegar
1 tablespoonful flour	$\frac{1}{2}$ pint water
1 teaspoonful salt	$\frac{1}{2}$ lb flaky pastry
$\frac{1}{2}$ teaspoonful pepper	milk or beaten egg to glaze

Remove the fat from the steak and cut the lean meat into $\frac{3}{4}$ inch cubes. Prepare the kidneys and cut into tiny cubes. Dip each piece into the flour. Melt the fat removed from the steak. Mince and add the onion, and fry gently for a few minutes; then put in the steak and kidney and stir constantly until the surface is well seared and browned. Remove to a stew-pan. Add the boiling water to the remaining fat, and strain. Add to this the salt and pepper, sauces, and vinegar, and pour over the meat. Cover tightly, and cook over a low heat until the meat is tender. Turn the meat into a pie-dish with a half-inch rim. It should be filled to the brim. Place a china funnel (or small earthen teacup turned upside down) in the middle, and leave the meat to get quite cold. Meanwhile strain off the gravy in the pan and thicken with a little flour. (A little butter may also be added.) Pour half of it over the meat. Cover with pastry, leaving a hole in the centre for the steam to escape; decorate, and brush with milk or beaten egg. Bake in a good oven for thirty minutes. Re-heat the rest of the gravy and pour into the pie through the funnel just before serving.

~ F Marian McNeill ~

A SPICE CUP FOR MACGREEGOR

$\frac{1}{4}$ pint pineapple juice	1 $\frac{1}{2}$ oz sugar
$\frac{1}{4}$ pint orange juice	1 tablespoon honey
$\frac{1}{4}$ pint grapefruit juice	4 cloves
$\frac{1}{3}$ pint water	$\frac{1}{4}$ teaspoon grated nutmeg
$\frac{1}{2}$ lemon	$\frac{1}{4}$ teaspoon cinnamon
$\frac{1}{8}$ teaspoon mixed spice	
2 pints ginger ale or Scottish aerated mineral water	

Add pineapple, orange and grapefruit juice to 1 $\frac{1}{2}$ gills of water. Add the grated rind and juice of the lemon, the sugar, honey and spices. Stand for 12 hours. Strain and add the ginger ale or mineral water.

~ Anon ~

ON HOGMANAY

Hou monie days are in a year?
Three hunder and saxty-five.
I've counted ilka ane o them
As shuir as I'm alive.

Ye'll see a ferlie at the Cross
That ye micht think is queer
– A man that has as monie nebs
As days are in the year.

Nou see if ye can tell me
And tell me true the day.
Hou monie noses on his face
Does that puir mannie hae?

ANSWER:
He has one nose. There are 365 days in a year,
but this is Hogmanay, and there is only one day
left in the year, *ie* this year.

~ *J K Annand* ~

PLEASE TAE HELP THE GUIZARDS
AND I'LL SING YE A BONNY WEE SANG

THE doings of the *guizards* (that is, masquers) form a conspicuous feature in the New-year proceedings throughout Scotland. The evenings on which these personages are understood to be privileged to appear, are those of Christmas, Hogmanay, New-year's Day, and Handsel Monday. Such of the boys as can pretend to anything like a voice, have for weeks before been thumbing the collection of excellent new songs, which lies like a bunch of rags in the window sole; and being now able to screech up *Barbara Allan,* or *The wee Cot-house and the wee Kail-yardie,* they determine upon enacting the part of guizards. For this purpose they don old shirts belonging to their fathers, and mount casques of brown paper, shaped so like a mitre, that I am tempted to believe them borrowed from the Abbot of Unreason: attached to this is a sheet of the same paper, which, falling down in front, covers and conceals the whole face, except where holes are made to let through the point of the nose, and afford sight to the eyes and breath to the mouth.

Each vocal guizard is, like a knight of old, attended by a kind of humble squire, who assumes the habiliments of a girl, with an old woman's cap and a broomstick, and is styled 'Bessie'. Bessie is equal in no respect, except that she shares fairly in the proceeds of the enterprise. She goes before her principal; opens all the doors at which he pleases to exert his singing powers; and busies herself, during the time of the song, in sweeping the floor with her broomstick, or in playing any other antics that she thinks may amuse the indwellers. The common reward of this entertainment is a halfpenny; but many churlish persons fall upon the unfortunate guizards, and beat them out of the house. Let such persons, however, keep a good watch upon their cabbage-gardens next Hallowe'en!

~ Robert Chambers ~

STOVIES FOR HOGMANAY

THE real celebration of the season was Hogmanay, which gave us a chance to stay up all night, dropping 'first footing' presents of coal or shortbread for our neighbours, and having a jolly good time wherever we visited. Everybody left their doors wide for anyone who wished to come in, and I remember trying to keep my eyes open as people trooped into our house from midnight onwards. Mum always had a big pot of 'stovies', mince and potatoes, bubbling away on the hob, and all sorts of people, friends and strangers, would wander in and out of our back door all night, exchanging greetings and having a 'dram' or two .... When we finally ventured out ourselves there was inevitably a flurry of snow on the way back, and we would be stuck in a drift a mile from home with not a welling- ton boot between the five of us. Year in, year out, Dad vowed never to go out again on Hogmanay.

As we grew older, Roger particularly enjoyed the fun, stay- ing out all night and staggering back at seven in the morning to feed the beasts before collapsing in his bed. Once I had passed my driving test when I was 17, I would act as driver to Roger and his friends; I don't like the taste or feel of alcohol, which is always rather convenient for other people on social occasions!

~ Evelyn Glennie ~

HOGMANAY FARE

THERE are two ways of celebrating Hogmanay in Scotland. When I was young we used to dance up to midnight until the church bell pealed out across the snow (I cannot remember Christmas in Angus without snow), then the toast was drunk to the New Year and a thumping good supper was served, usually a choice of hot roast chicken with baked or boiled ham, and all the trimmings, and cold game or pork pie with jacket potatoes, followed by luscious creams, such as Stone Cream, a super trifle and hot mince pies and Athole Brose. Black Bun, Shortie and tea always followed later on because the dance lasted until cock crow. Nowadays it is more usual to invite a few friends in for the occasion and serve a buffet supper ....

At Hogmanay, various drinks used to be offered on the Braes of Angus, such as port wine and whisky. In the Highlands Athole Brose sometimes took the place of both for the toast. Nowadays, it is more usual to start with sherry and drink a cider or wine cup throughout the meal, and offer champagne or port wine for the toast, but when there are men present there is always whisky in the offing.

~ Elizabeth Craig ~

BAKED HAM
(Method particularly suited to strongly flavoured hams)

INGREDIENTS:

2 lb gammon (middle, corner or hock)
1 oz soft brown sugar
cloves

SERVINGS: 6–8

TIME AND TEMPERATURE:

1-1½ hours. Oven temperature: 375° F, no. 5 position in oven, middle shelf.

METHOD:

1   Wash ham and soak several hours.
2   Calculate cooking time, allowing 20 minutes per lb and an extra 20 minutes.
3   Boil the ham for half the time.
4   Remove ham from water and cool for ½ hour.
5   Wrap completely in cooking foil and bake in moderate oven for remainder of time.
6   About 15 minutes before cooking is complete, remove foil and skin the ham.
7   Score the fat in diamonds, stud with cloves and dredge heavily with brown sugar.
8   Return to the oven for 15 minutes.

NOTE: A whole ham may be cooked in the same way, allowing only 20 minutes per lb.

~ Glasgow and West of Scotland College of Domestic Science ~

CLARET CUP

To each bottle of Burgundy or claret add 1 glass of sherry and 1 liqueur glass of orange Curacao, lemon peel cut very thin, and 2 tablespoons caster sugar to each bottle used. Let this remain a short time on ice. Just before serving add 2 bottles of soda water (splits). Decorate with fresh mint.

~ Kenneth Ireland ~

STONE CREAM

apricot jam
juice of 1 lemon
1 wineglass sherry
1 pint cream
2 oz caster sugar

1 teaspoon vanilla essence
$^1/_2$ oz gelatine
2 tablespoons water
$^1/_4$ pint hot milk

Spread the bottom of a glass dish with apricot jam. Pour in the lemon juice and sherry. Bring the cream to a boil. Stir in caster sugar and vanilla essence. When sugar is dissolved, leave until cool. Soften the gelatine in the water. Add milk. Stir till dissolved. Cool slightly, then stir in the cream. Leave until nearly cold, then pour carefully over the jam. Serves 6.

NOTE:

In some parts of Scotland, $^1/_2$ lb apricot jam is used, and only 2oz is spread over the bottom of dish. Cover with a layer of the cooled cream, then chill till set. Spread with 2oz more of the jam, then cover with another layer of cream. Repeat layers.

~ Elizabeth Craig ~

SYLLABUB

1 pint cream
juice of 2 lemons

$^1/_2$ lb sugar
glass of sherry or white wine

Whisk until stiff. Put in sundae glasses and stand in cold place for 12 hours.

~ Scottish Women's Rural Institutes ~

ATHOLE BROSE

Strain a handful of oatmeal through a fine sieve into a basin, and mix with cold water till the consistency of a thick paste. Be careful not to make it too watery. Add 4 dessertspoons of run honey to 4 sherry glasses of the sieved oatmeal. Stir well together and put into a quart bottle. Fill up with whisky. Shake well before serving.

Can be drunk at once, or kept indefinitely if well corked and sealed. The bottle should be kept standing upright. Some ladies like a little cream added to it immediately before serving.

~ His Grace the Duke of Athole ~

YEAR'S END

The bonnie birds are winged and gaen,
Yowes hug the dykes like driven sna;
The anely cry that rings the rigs,
The brukken caa'in o the craw.

An cauldly cruel's the win that cuts,
The birks sae barely dreepin,
Its wail's as awesome as a wake,
As if the lan itself wis greetin,
A door on creakin hinges set,
The auld an New Year's meetin.

Syne simmer days an simmer thochts,
Are deid leaves blawn an dwined,
As life an daith, thimsels they mirl,
Foriver intertwined,
Future's unkent; the Past is past;
Bit sairly present till the mind.

Like Birth itsel we canna tell,
If hairst will follow breirin,
The winter smore that furls the door,
Is fite as hope, as dark as leavin,
The young fowk blythely forrit step,
The auld anes, latchy, grievin.

~ Sheena Blackhall ~

NEW YEAR'S DAY

~ Music by *James Stewart Roberston* ~

1st JANUARY – NE'ERDAY

NE'ERDAY. New Year observances included the keeping in of the last year's fire, first-footing, the giving of gifts, the mixing of *het-pints*, the drawing of the first water from the well, shinty, and other ball-games.

~ David Murison from *The Scottish Year ~*

From HOGMANAY

When ice has gruppit burn an' syke,
An' frosty roads gie cairters fike;
When cranreuch pouthers ilka dyke,
    An' white's the yairdie,
Let them haud Christmastide wha like –
    Scotland hauds Ne'erday.

~ W D Cocker ~

From THE TWA DOGS

That *merry day* the year begins,
They bar the door on frosty win's;
The nappy reeks wi' mantling ream,
An' sheds a heart-inspiring steam;
The luntan pipe, an' sneeshum mill,
Are handed round wi' right guid will;
The cantie, auld folks, crackan crouse,
The young anes rantan thro' the house –
My heart has been sae fain to see them,
That I for joy hae *barket* wi' them.

~ Robert Burns ~

NEW YEAR'S DAY IN PERTH

NEW Year's Day has always been held in Perth as a day of special hilarity. The festivities commenced on the evening of the last night of the old year. In addition to a sufficient supply of stimulants, each family provided a quantity of *carls*. These were oatmeal cakes of a triangular shape, prepared with treacle or other condiments. The whole circle of acquaintance visited for carls; and each individual had to sing for his supper, or at least for his cake. This practice has greatly fallen off; none but a rabble of children, called 'Guisards', now maintain the custom. New Year's morning was ushered in by a dram from the gudewife's bottle. It was then the practice to wait up for what was called the cream of the well – the fortunate damsel who succeeded in getting the first water of the year, being assured of a good husband before the end of it. The streets were crowded all night, by parties wishing to see what was going on, and by others on their way to call upon acquaintances. The ordinary restraints of society were thrown aside; and every man claimed the privilege of kissing any woman he chanced to meet ....

The changes which took place in trade about 1780, brought a great number of spinners and cloth printers to this neighbourhood, who introduced the custom of hot pints. On going to the houses of their friends, as first foot, they took with them a tea kettle full of a warm mixture of ale, whisky, and sugar; and as the visitor had also to do honour to the host's bottle, the parties, long before daylight, found they had taken rather more than enough.

~ George Penny ~

GRANNIE'S NEW YEAR

ON New Year morning I always took Grannie down to see her 'chum' a short tram ride away. But before we went, we made sure the room was tidied up, and the tables reset with the food and the wines for the folk who would drop in during the day to wish us a Happy New Year. My mother would be at home to welcome them, for she didn't have to go to work on New Year's Day, which was always a holiday.

I helped Grannie to put on her good black shoes, and I fastened the pin of the black cameo she wore at the neck of her best black silk blouse, and saw that the blouse was tucked in right the way round inside the waist of her long dark grey skirt. Then on top went her dark coat, and last of all her hat with its winter trimming of cherries was set carefully on her silvery hair, at an angle which wouldn't disturb the wee bun at the back. She looked entirely different from our workaday Grannie, and I was transformed from my schoolday self in my navy blue reefer coat, long black stockings and, best of all, *shoes* not boots. The shoes, I felt, gave me a most ladylike appearance. My black velour hat was held on with a good piece of elastic, which kept it firmly anchored at windy corners, and my curls were brushed neatly over my shoulders. When we reached the tram, where it stood waiting at the terminus, there always seemed to be a drunk man sitting inside, half-asleep, softly singing 'The Star o' Rabbie Burns', and for ever afterwards I always associated the name of Burns with New Year revelries ....

We told the conductor where to let us off, and he stopped the tram long enough to let us get down without splashing our stockings or Grannie's skirt, and then we crossed the road to the tenement where Grannie's chum lived. We reached a beautifully polished door on the landing and rang the bell. A soft shuffle told us she was coming, and then I was being embraced in a flurry of soft arms and incredibly soft face and we were bustled into the kitchen. At this time Grannie was about sixty and her friend about seventy-five, so she seemed truly ancient to me. She wore a snowy white cap with a fluted frill, and her black dress was protected by a large white apron. When she spoke, her voice was so soft I had to lean right forward to hear what she said. She might have stepped straight out of the pages of *Little Red Riding Hood* and I was fascinated. She in her turn was filled with wonder over me, and how lively I was, and how quick, and she kept turning and looking at me again and again as she got out plates and glasses and wine.

The kitchen was full of knick-knacks and shining brass, and there were little lace covers on all her chairs. Occasionally, to Grannie's horror, I seized the poker as a prop when I sang them a song from a pantomime, but their favourite was 'Bonnie Mary of Argyle' which always brought a tear to their eyes ....

There was an old-fashioned horn gramophone which wheezed out the songs of Harry Lauder, and I'd reduce the two old ladies to scandalised laughter when I imitated him afterwards. It must have been a long time since the old lady had entertained children, for she seemed to have no idea of what was suitable. I was handed a glass of port to sip when she poured out one for Grannie and herself. Grannie either didn't notice or was too polite to interfere, and I was forced to take tiny sips of this horrid-tasting liquid and pretend it was as nice as my mother's delicious ginger wine. Later, the strong tea nearly took the skin off my tongue, and Grannie frowned at me when I screwed up my nose. But the sandwiches and cakes were delicious, although the two old ladies didn't seem to have much interest in them. I was amazed that they seemed to get more pleasure from that terrible wine and the strong tea.

Afterwards, I brought Grannie home, taking great care to see that she got on and off the tramcars safely. She only went out twice a year, at the Fair and at Hogmanay, so she wasn't used to traffic. I nearly burst with pride at being her escort, and we had to stop every few yards for the neighbours to admire her outfit and to wish her 'Happy New Year'. When we got home her lovely shoes were put away in their cardboard box. Her coat was hung up and left to air before being stowed at the back of the wardrobe, where it would stay until it was brought out for her to wear at the Fair. Her skirt was folded over a hanger, the black silk blouse put away with tissue paper, and there was my dear familiar Grannie again, picking up her knitting needles and getting on with a sock while she told my mother all about our outing. When my mother asked if I'd behaved myself, I held my breath and wondered if Grannie would mention how free I had been with the poker, but she just glanced at me, and assured my mother, 'Oh aye, she did fine. She's quite gettin' to be the lady'.

~ Molly Weir ~

KIRKWALL TO THE BA'

UNTIL early this century, the favourite New Year's Day sport in Orkney was football playing. 'In the various fields of play,' comments John Robertson, 'there were no sides, touchlines or goals ... and an inflated bladder of a cow, sheep or pig, encased in leather and usually fashioned by the local cobbler, was lustily kicked about in a rough and tumble on the parish Ba' Green.' Out of such a game ... there gradually developed in the late eighteenth century and the first half of the nineteenth, the Kirkwall Ba' Game .... So energetic is this game that, in the old part of the town through which it is played, houses and shops have their windows and doors stoutly barricaded.

The contest takes place on ... Christmas Day and New Year's Day .... From the mercat cross in front of St Magnus Cathedral, a cork-filled ball is thrown, on the stroke of 1 o'clock, to the expectant group of men waiting in the Broad Street. Before the game is over, more than a hundred players may take part, representing the opposing halves of the original town. Those born to the south of the Cathedral are Up-the-Gates and those born to the north of it Doon-the-Gates ....

The aim of both Uppies and Doonies ... is to carry the ball against all opposition to their own end of the town, the waters of the harbour being the recognised goal of the Doonies, and the crossroads at the opposite side of Kirkwall the goal of the Uppies. Their object is attained by pushing, so that the players almost immediately form a tight scrum, bracing themselves against the walls of the houses. In their midst, locked in determined arms, is the ball. On either side of it ... the players face each other and push. Although it is so hot in the centre of the scrum that steam rises in a thin cloud on the winter air, and … forceful tactics are required, tempers are usually held in check and foul play is not tolerated.

There are no rules, but skilful co-ordination may give one of the sides an advantage, and players conserve their strength for violent surges by periods of apparent inaction. The hundreds of spectators who follow the progress of the game often have to scatter quickly, for the scrum is always liable to erupt, and there is swirling disorder until it forms again a little way along the street. A good game may last for several hours, even after the short winter daylight has disappeared. Weight of numbers tells in the end, and the last few yards to the goal may be covered at a cracking pace. When Kirkwall Harbour is the goal attained, it is obligatory to throw the ball into the sea. Several players invariably plunge in after it. The leather 'ba'', handmade for the contest, is a coveted trophy. It is always awarded by popular acclamation to some player who has been a notable participant over a period of years, and … made his presence felt in the game just ended.

While there is no evidence that the game … existed before the nineteenth century, tales of the traditional rivalry which existed between the two sections of the town are persistent …. A favourite tale is of a local tyrant called Tusker, who was pursued and killed near Perth by an enterprising Orcadian. As the victor brought the severed head of Tusker home to Kirkwall, swinging from the pommel of his saddle, the tyrant's protruding teeth broke the skin of his leg. Poisoning set in, and the young champion had no sooner reached the mercat cross, and flung the head to the crowd … than he died. With mingled grief and anger the townsfolk kicked the head of the odious Tusker around the street, thus initiating, the legend says, Kirkwall's Ba' Game.

~ *Ernest Marwick* ~

THE BA'

THE Kirkwall New Year's Ba' is a survival of the ancient rivalry between Church and State, between King's men and Bishop's men. Until near the end of the Fifteenth Century, that part of the town which lies to the south of what is now Post Office Lane was regarded as the Episcopal domain, and called the Laverock; the Burgh proper, the secular part, extended from Broad Street northwards to the sea.

If you love a democratic, acrobatic, half-aquatic
    Game of football, with ten rules, or none at all,
Then you'd better take a train, then a boat to cross the main,
    And land on New Year's Day at Old Kirkwall.

Put on your cast-off clothes, and if you love your toes,
    A pair of seaboots helps in the stramash;
Throw all your dignitee away into the Peerie Sea;
    Don't bring your watch, though none will steal your cash.

Then take your proper place, minus frock-coat and sleek 'lum'.
    On Broad Street nearing one, and keep an eye
Upon the crawling clock; when it rings you'll get a shock!
    Up leaps the Ba', and then it's do or die!

For the game may last an hour, yet it's far beyond the power
    Of mortal man to give an estimate;
It may run for half a day, or ten minutes end the fray
    In favour of the Up- or Doon-the-Gate.

*   *   *

The Doonies all push north, while the Uppies, topsy-turve,
    Strive to take the precious leather to the south;
The one goal's Kirkwall Bay, the other, lackaday!
    Is a ruined castle, gnarled and uncouth.

*   *   *

Where is the famous ball? Well, that's often hard to tell,
    But it's somewhere in the middle of the throng,
Where the steam uprises most. Yes, sometimes it does get lost.
    But just listen to the magic of its song!

You can hear its breakers roar, as they did in days of yore;
    None resist it, neither high nor low degree;
They're obedient to the call of this New Year's festival,
    To this thousand-throated summons of the sea.

*   *   *

The Vikings, brave and bold, with their helms of burnished gold,
    Played this game in days now hidden in the haze;
And our ancient minster brown, overlooking Kirkwall Town,
    Agrees that men don't change their little ways.

~ David Horne ~

HANDSEL MONDAY

HANDSEL MONDAY:

'The first Monday of the New Year; so called because it has been the custom from time immemorial, for servants and others to ask or receive handsel on this day.'

~ John Jamieson from Dictionary of the Scottish Language, 1818 ~

'As to holidays for recreation or merry-making, the people have only one in the year, called Handsel Monday.'

~ David Murison from First Statistical Account ~

OVER sixty years ago I worked in a lawyer's office. The building was part of what was once known as the New Town of Edinburgh, as opposed to the Old Town which was built on the spine of the Royal Mile. It was a gracious dwelling with a wide stone staircase leading up four storeys and surmounted by a magnificent cupola.

I remember round about Christmas Eve hearing footsteps on the stairs and a young male voice shouting, 'Please for the Roll Boy's Handsel! Please for the Roll Boy's Handsel!' This was the young boy who delivered daily the 'Rolls' or lists of cases to be heard at the Court of Session.

Ten or fifteen years ago the Christmas Box, as it was called, was discontinued and indeed there have not been any Roll Boys for the last five years.

~ Marjorie Wilson ~

HANDSEL Monday in Perth was the principal day with the working classes. By one in the morning the streets were in an uproar with young people, who appeared to consider themselves privileged to do whatever mischief they pleased.

It was a constant practice to pull down sign boards, or any thing that came in the way, and make a large bonfire with them at the cross, – all being for the benefit of trade, and the support of the good old customs. Numbers of boys, belonging to the Glover Incorporation, were to be heard in every quarter selling small purses at a half-penny each; these were made of the parings of leather, and enabled the lads to gather something to hold Handsel Monday with. They were generally all sold off early in the morning. The tradesmen were all idle this day, and considered themselves entitled to handsel from their employers; and even from individuals in any way connected with the business. Thus the weavers, having received their handsel from the manufacturer, a deputation from the shop was sent to the wright who made their utensils; another to the reed-maker, and to the chandler who supplied them with candles; and a third to the company who boiled the yarn. The whole proceeds of these begging commissions were put together and spent in the evening in a tavern.

~ George Penny ~

HANDSEL MONDAY 1926

Hip! Hip! Hooray for Handsel Monday!
I'll hae pennies in ma pooch the day!
There's five bob for the postie wha brings us oor mail,
A hauf-croun for the fishwife wi her muckle creel;
The same for the milkman that comes at seeven o'clock,
Florins for the dustmen that tak awa the brock,
Twa shillings for the fairmer wi his cairt o neeps an spuds,
An shuggar for his Dobbin as up the brae he thuds;
A tanner for the paper-boy, an a shinin threepenny bit;
The rag-wife gets a bowl o broth – an she's fine pleased wi it;
A puckle tea, some baby clouts for the tinkler wife –
She gies me paper flooers, an a blessing for a lang an happy life.

The next ane's special, for the lame ex-serviceman;
A crumpie, new pun note, forbye a dram.

A shilling for the grocer's loon, whustlin on his bike,
An the auld man wi the trumpet – ye've never heard his like!
He gets a reamin mutton pie, an a screw-top o guid beer,
While the mannie howkin up the street maun aye hae his New Year –
An orange an a daud o cake, twa mince pies for his tea,
An in ma daddie's pocket? – Three new pennies aa for me!

~ Marjory Greig ~

EFTER HOGMANAY

Big an' sma' shops screechin' 'Sale',
An' maist nae siller left tae buy.
'Scandal o' auld fowk freezin',',
Newsboys cry,
An' ilka body sneezin'.
Scots vow, as they hae dune for mony a day,
Tae spend a get sicht less next Hogmany.

~ Jamie A Smith ~

JACK FROST (1)

Come gie a cheer
Jack Frost is here!

Lang may be bide
This wintertide.

Sune lochs will bear
And we'll be there

To slide and skate
Baith air and late

Sae gie a cheer
Jack Frost is here!

JACK FROST (2)

Jack Frost
Get lost!

I feel the cauld
Nou that I'm auld.

Cauld maks me seik,
Banes grane and creak.

My neb turns blae
My fingers tae

Get lost
Jack Frost.

~ J K Annand ~

NEW YEAR'S WEATHER

AT length, Edinburgh, with her satellite hills and all the sloping country, are sheeted up in white. If it has happened in the dark hours, nurses pluck their children out of bed and run with them to some commanding window, whence they may see the change that has been worked upon earth's face. 'A' the hills are covered wi' snaw,' they sing, 'and Winter's noo come fairly!' And the children, marvelling at the silence and the white landscape, find a spell appropriate to the season in the words. The reverberation of the snow increases the pale daylight, and brings all objects nearer the eye. The Pentlands are smooth and glittering, with here and there the black ribbon of a dry-stone dyke, and here and there, if there be wind, a cloud of blowing snow upon a shoulder. The Firth seems a leaden creek, that a man might almost jump across, between well-powdered Lothian and well-powdered Fife. And the effect is not, as in other cities, a thing of half a day; the streets are soon trodden black, but the country keeps its virgin white; and you have only to lift your eyes and look over miles of country snow. An indescribable cheerfulness breathes about the city; and the well-fed heart sits lightly and beats gaily in the bosom. It is New-year's weather ....

Of old, Edinburgh University was the scene of heroic snow-balling; and one riot obtained the epic honours of military intervention. But the great generation, I am afraid, is at an end; and even during my own college days, the spirit appreciably declined. Skating and sliding, on the other hand, are honoured more and more; and curling, being a creature of the national genius, is little likely to be disregarded. The patriotism that leads a man to eat Scotch bun will scarce desert him at the curling-pond. Edinburgh, with its long steep pavements, is the proper home of sliders; many a happy urchin can slide the whole way to school; and the profession of errand boy is transformed into a holiday amusement. As for skating, there is scarce any city so handsomely provided. Duddingstone Loch lies under the abrupt southern side of Arthur's Seat; in summer, a shield of blue, with swans sailing from the reeds; in winter, a field of ringing ice. The village church sits above it on a green promontory; and the village smoke rises from among goodly trees .... On the opposite side of the loch, the ground rises to Craigmillar ....

It is worth a climb, even in summer, to look down upon the loch from Arthur's Seat; but it is tenfold more so on a day of skating. The surface is thick with people moving easily and swiftly and leaning over at a thousand graceful inclinations; the crowd opens and closes and keeps moving through itself like water, and the ice rings to half a mile away, with the flying steel. As night draws on, the single figures melt into the dusk, until only an obscure stir and coming and going of black clusters, is visible upon the loch. A little longer, and the first torch is kindled and begins to flit rapidly across the ice in a ring of yellow reflection, and this is followed by another and another, until the whole field is full of skimming lights.

~ Robert Louis Stevenson ~

HEIGH-HO FOR
WINTER DAYS AND SNOW!

ON the return of the boys to the hospital they all seemed to have enjoyed themselves thoroughly ....

The snow was still on the ground to the depth of nearly two feet, having fallen very heavily during the holidays. Now was the time to punish the detestable 'tellers', who had made their companions suffer in many instances for very slight offences, their only desire being to get into favour with the wardsmen or other officials, who often received information from them quite unasked. There are few school-boys who do not hate the very name of 'tell-tale' and who do not entertain a most thorough dislike for those who bear it. But in Heriot's Hospital the tell-tale was looked upon rather in the light of a criminal, who was not only detested but was punished at every opportunity.

For the first day or two after the holidays the educational department was not quite so rigorously carried on as usual; and as the boys were encouraged rather than otherwise in larking amongst the snow, full freedom was given to them in the greens. In fact they were allowed to do pretty much as they pleased, within rational bounds. Sides were chosen and snowballing was indulged in until all were tired out.

Then they set to to make huge snowballs, with which a snowhouse was built, leaving a small doorway to be closed up with other material at hand. A search was made for two or three of the tellers who had distinguished themselves during the 'half'. When they had been captured they were pushed into the snowhouse, crying and struggling, and the door blocked up. It was no jerrybuilt fabric either, but a strong and solid prison, and by the time the unfortunates managed to see daylight again, they were both tired and sore. No doubt they would think twice before incurring the risk of having themselves put into the same place again.

Next day the snowhouse was rebuilt in the model of a fort, and the battle of the 'seventh greens' was fought, with the lawds in the fort and the cholds and knaps as the attacking party; the fight was both fierce and long, and it was hard to say who had gained the victory. At last a cheer rang out, in unison with the Wark dinner bell calling the knaps to their 'tout-soup', to which they did ample justice that day.

When they reached the square they found Dr Bedford standing in conversation with some one at Mammie's 'connie'. One of the knaps conceived the notion of trying to see how the Doctor would take a 'taste of the weather'. Accordingly he let fly a snowball which whizzed past the Doctor's head and flattened itself on the chapel wall. The Doctor took no notice, which gave encouragement to another little chap who tried a second shot. This time the aim was more precise, as the Doctor's soft 'wide-awake' testified. Turning round with a smile on his face, Dr Bedford was about to remark that he was satisfied, or something to that effect, when two or three more let fly at once. Seeing that the time was not one for parley (and it was not in the Doctor to be ill-natured), he gathered his cloak about his ears and made over the square to his own quarters. On reaching the Govies' door, he turned to the boys and rewarded them with a playful shake of the head; after which he immediately disappeared. It was well for him that he did, for the door which he had just shut showed in a moment what he would have got. This evidence of good feeling on the part of Dr Bedford told with marked effect upon the boys, who were jubilant over their little bit of fun.

~ Jamieson Baillie ~

LAMPLIGHT, MOONLIGHT
AND THE GLINT OF ICE

WE didn't have skate-boards or even skates in the 1920s and 30s. But in winter there were slides stretching the whole length of mile-long meadow walks from Melville Drive to the Royal Infirmary, shining golden from street lamps and a wintry moon.

You joined the queue and mingled steaming breath with the unknown, the dimly glimpsed faces, clutching hands and unfamiliar voices filling the night with thuds and yells and laughter until suddenly all was obliterated by scattered salt and a glowering policeman.

With a sledge and a brother-in-law for escort we piled one on top of the other in a sweating, yelling mass, bodies flying off at intervals, others landing in the whins at the bottom of Blackford Hill. I carried the black 'prin whickles', as I called them, embedded in my knees for many a long year.

When we finally got the longed-for boots and skates, skating was different and more sophisticated. Blackford Pond was exciting enough, but nothing ever excelled the evening expeditions to Thriepmuir Reservoir in the Pentland Hills. Out by bus to Balerno, then the long two-mile walk uphill in the dark past the mansionhouse of Marchbanks; although there always seemed to be a moon turning the stretch of frozen water to a great milky pearl clasped in a setting of quiet hills. Here laughter and voices were muted as boots were laced and figures stumbled or glided away into the distance, hissing blades scoring keen runnels in the ice. As soon as you stopped, the air became almost too painful to breathe and the silence was broken by the startled cry of a wild duck or by ominous cracks as the frost tightened its grip. Or was the ice cracking up? We were never quite sure, but it all added to the thrill of excitement.

Later there was the Ice Rink at Haymarket where we waltzed, pirouetted, crossed hands and showed off to the strains of an orchestra playing 'The Skaters' Waltz' or 'Tales from the Vienna Woods', our short flared skirts fluttering like flower petals.

But nothing can ever eradicate the simple joys of childhood and it is with a deep abiding delight that we remember the earlier youthful pleasures.

~ Marjorie Wilson ~

SNAWMAN

We soopit and we shovelled
And made a man o snaw
Wi chuckie stanes for buttons
For een and neb ana.

We gied him Geordie's gravat
And Grandpa's auld lum hat,
We even borrowed Father's pipe
– Did he no girn at that!

And ilka ane that saw him
Declared that he looked braw,
But och! the thowe cam far owre quick
And meltit him awa.

~ J K Annand ~

THE ROARIN' GAME

A cauldrife sun keeks ower the hill,
Shines on the snaw it canna thowe,
An' sparkles on the scruntit birks
That gaird the lochan in the howe.
There curlers to the ice hae ta'en,
While winter hauds the land in grip,
An' clear upon the frosty air
I hear the voice o' Jock, their skip –
The weel-kent voice that aft I hear
Shout to his collie on the hill.
I pause an' listen to his cries,
His exhortations lood an' shrill.
'Hey, Tammas, can ye see this stane?
Weel, dunt it oot noo; here's the port.
I like ye, aye, I like ye fine.
Soop, soop 'er up! Eh, man, ye're short!
Weel, try again then, elbow oot.
Can ye get roon'? That's no' sae bad.
Ye're comin', dod! Ye'll get'm – dune!
You for the curler, Tammas lad.'
He wrings puir Tammas by the haun'.
His neive can gi'e a frichtsome grip.
Oh! wae betide the denty loof
That gets a shake frae Jock the skip.
He gi'es nae praise that's no' weel-earned,
An' whiles he proves an unco rager;
He'd flyte upon the laird himsel'
Gin he was no' weel up, I'se wager.
'Noo, Doctor, juist a canny shot.
Ye see this stane? well, chap an' lie.
Soop, soop like bleezes, fine, sir, fine! –
Man, but this roarin' mak's me dry!'
It's aye a "roarin' game" wi' Jock,
His voice could droon a clap o' thun'er.
A guid shot gars him loup for joy,
A bad ane gars him grue wi' scunner.
'Can ye get through atween thae twa?
Aye, pit your specs on, Doctor Chisholm.

Gey weel laid doon! she'll come hersel'.
Haud aff there, canny wi' the besom!'
But noo the mirk is fa'in fast,
The lichts are gleamin' in the clachan;
The inn-door, sweein' wide agee,
Lets oot a burst o' merry lauchin'.
'Aye, this maun be oor hinmaist en'.
We've bate ye fair an' square, I'se war'n:
An, gin it doesna thowe ower nicht,
Ye'll yet your licks again the morn.'

~ W D Cocker ~

5th JANUARY –
TWELFTH NIGHT or AULD YULE
(Old Christmas Eve)

OLD CHRISTMAS IN SHETLAND

OLD Christmas on January 6th is still being celebrated in part of the most northerly islands of Scotland, the Shetlands. At one time New Christmas, as it was then called, was simply ignored; it seems that the islanders resented such a change as they clung to the well known and loved ways of their fathers.

In the course of my lifetime and during the early part of the present century, I have heard the bells of Christmas 'Ring out the old, ring in the new' in no uncertain tones.

With the coming of radio and later, television, young people's minds, which are readily imitative, were presented in sound and vision with the merry bells of Christmas as celebrated over the British Isles; so, slowly but surely, the change came about, for it was inconvenient to be out of step with friends overseas. Some of the older folks, loath to lose memories of the happy Christmas Days of the past, still kept a warm place in their hearts for the sixth day of January and made holiday then.

In our youth, my brother and I worked in my father's grocer's shop in Scalloway, and I can recall just how busy we were during the first week of each new year, when small boats arrived from all the nearby islands to stock up provender for the Christmas celebrations on January 6th.

In the small hamlets of east and West Quarff which lie about three miles from Scalloway, a brilliant little ceremony used to be held to welcome Old Christmas morning: quantities of candles were bought from us, to be displayed in every window, so that the whole valley of Quarff was alight early in the darkness of Christmas morn. Today we see many Christmas trees draped in coloured lights in windows everywhere – a lovely gesture, brought forward from the past.

It seems that the only district in Shetland now celebrating Old Christmas is the Island of Foula which lies about twenty-six miles seaward from Scalloway – a rocky bastion with cliffs among the highest in Britain and carrying a population of forty. In winter when seas are usually heavy, Foula used to be cut off, and supplies and mail arrived late. Today, with Loganair touching down at all the outlying islands, Foula is no longer suffering its winter isolation and receives its Christmas mail in good time for both New and Old Christmas. The people of Foula hold both January 6th and 7th as Christmas, when friends are entertained and tasty dishes are prepared for visitors, while with the playing of 'The Shaalds of Foula' and other well known dance and fiddle tunes the hearts of young and old are lightened. (The Shaalds are the shallow fishing grounds where the islanders take their catch of fine white fish.)

Among the older Shetlanders who now celebrate New Christmas as the accepted festival, I should imagine that when New Christmas is over, the past still holds them so strongly in ties of memory that they take up the fiddle on Old Christmas Night and uncork a wee dram, so making the best of both occasions!

~ Clement J Williamson ~

6th JANUARY –
UPHALLIDAY
or EPIPHANY
(The end of the Twelve Days of Yule)

THE STAR

After the tumult of the sunset colours,
    Crimson and gold has faded o'er the sea,
Clasped, gemlike in the mantle of the evening,
    A star shines steadily.

And there, though gales should rise and dark clouds gather,
  And lightning flames should flash from hill to hill,
Beyond the storm-rack and the thunderous darkness
  The star is shining still.

~ Vagaland ~

From MATTHEW'S VERSION
OF THE STORY OF THE GOOD NEWS

WHEN Jesus had been born in Bethlehem in Judaea, in the time of King Herod, there came to Jerusalem from the East scholars who were students of the stars. 'Where,' they asked, 'is the newly born King of the Jews? We are looking for him, because we have seen his star rise, and we have come to do homage to him.' When King Herod heard about this he was alarmed, and all Jerusalem shared his alarm. So he called a meeting of the chief priests and the experts in the Law, and tried to find out from them where the Messiah was to be born. 'In Bethlehem in Judaea,' they told him, 'for scripture through the prophet says:

> "And you Bethlehem, in land of Judah,
> are by no means the least of the leaders of Judah,
> for from you there shall emerge
> the leader who will be the shepherd of my people Israel."'

Then Herod secretly sent for the scholars from the East, and carefully questioned them about the date when the star had appeared. He sent them to Bethlehem. 'Go,' he said, 'and make every effort to trace the child. And, when you have found him, send word to me, for I too wish to go and do homage to him.' When they heard what the King had to say, they set out, and the star, which they had seen when it first rose, led them on, until it came and stopped where the little child was. And very great was their rejoicing when they saw the star. They went into the house and they saw the little child with Mary his mother, and they knelt down and did him homage. They unpacked their treasures, and offered him gifts, gold, frankincense and myrrh. Because a message from God came to them in a dream, warning them not to go back to Herod, they returned to their own country by another way.

~ William Barclay ~

DA TREE KINGS

Dey wir a king in Jorsalaland
    At heard a windros tell
Aboot a bairn at wis boarn ta be
    Far heicher as himsell.

'What tell is dis at ye bring ta me?
    Fir I am hale an feer,
An wha daar say at I sanna rule
    Fir lang an mony a year?'

Dan answered him his servant-man,
    Shakkin fae fit ta head,
'Oh, hit wis tree queer boddies
    At kyentna what dey said.'

'Whatn folk wis du spaekin til?
    My man, du sall answer me;
Or du sall get dy head i dy haand,
    An dy lugs ta play dee wi.'

'Weel, as fir dem, believe you me,
    At een wis as black as sin,
An een shörely hed da gulsa
    Be da colour o his skyin.

Da treed wis a kinda grey-faced man,
    An he hed da queerest een –
A mair raised-laek, örie boddie
    A'm shöre A'm never seen.'

'Ye'll geng an fin yun uncan men
    Afore dey seek dir haem,
An tell dem at da king o da laand
    Wid spaek a wird wi dem.'

Da servant-man göd furt ta seek,
    An hit wisna lang ava
Till a staavin man fae Serkland
    Cam strampin in ida Haa.

An a man fae far-aff Asaland,
    Wi his head aa filled wi laer,
An aa da wisdom o da Aest,
    Followed him in trowe dere.

An a king fae a nordern kyuntrie,
    Wi grey-blue draemin een –
Dey stöd afore King Herod,
    Sae stately ta be seen.

An Herod da King he set him up
    An sat an spak dem fair,
An he listened as da Tree Wise Men
    Telled what wis brocht dem dere.

An Herod da King, he faased dem up
    An baad dem geng an see;
'An mind at, whin ye're fun da bairn,
    Ye'll bring da wird ta me.'

Dan up got Gaspar an Melchior,
    An up got Baltasar,
Dey left da Haa o Herod da King,
    An göd apo da Star.

Da Star at stöd ower Bethlehem,
    Da place whaar Mary lay;
An, whin dey fan da Peerie King,
    Ta Him dir gifts dey gae.

Dey widna geng back ta Herod da King,
    Nedder fir drink or maet;
Dey widna trust da Bairn ta him,
    So dey took anidder gaet.

*   *   *

An folk is waitit twa thoosand year,
    Ida hoops at, shön or late,
Da kings an da rulers o da wirld,
    Will aa geng anidder gaet.

                    ~ Vagaland ~

YULE'S COME AND YULE'S GANE

A T the turn of the New Year we dismantled the tree, put away the ornaments, took down the greenery, and folded the paper chains, bells and lanterns concertina-wise ready to hang another day.

We had no balloons left, for their brief glory ended with a pop on a sprig of holly.

~ Amy Stewart Fraser ~

The magic of the New Year lasted quite a long time, with even the postman being invited in for a glass of something and a piece of cake. But we knew it was over when one day we went into the room and the tablecloth and the food had vanished. It was back to school for us then, and back to the workaday world for the tenement, but our pleasure in the Hogmanay revels kept us warm for many a long winter day afterwards. In the tenements we accepted cheerfully that it had to be auld claes and parritch after the feasting.

~ Molly Weir ~

YULE'S COME AND YULE'S GANE

Yule's come and Yule's gane
And we hae feasted weel,
Sae Jock maun to his flail again
And Jenny to her wheel.

The snaw's saftly fallin
But bairns to schule maun gang,
O Winter, Winter, flee awa,
Let Simmer come again!

~ Words and music: *traditional* ~

E P I L O G U E

SECOND CHRISTMAS

Christ cam at Christmas,
joy tae his midder's hert,
joy tae a world
at didna want ta ken;
only da shepherds saw
(waakrife an kinda faert)
sometin by-ordnar
tae da sight o men:

gadderie o angels
movin as dancers shift,
tellin Heeven's high news
fae da upper air,
an da great star at stüde
low i da aest lift,
shawin whaar da Bairn lay
in a manger dere.

Nane took muckle notice,
'less tree wise men,
at cam, saw, marvelled, an
gaed hame anidder wye –
for Herod wis ampin,
wid a hed da Bairn taen,
torn fae his midder's scurt
ere he hed time ta cry!

Bit his time wisna come;
he hed time ta grow tall,
attend his Faider's business,
geng at last ta Calvary!
Aa dat wis ida future –
noo wis a coo's stall,
on dis blissed Christmas,
da first in history!

Nane kens da time o year –
voar, hairst, black nights,
ün o a simmer air,
snawy day or green –
bit whin Christ in his glory
comes ta pit da world ta rights,
dey'll truly be a Christmas
da laek wis never seen!

~ Stella Sutherland ~

G L O S S A R Y

aa	all	bates	beats
aabodie	everybody	bauchles	old shoes
aafil	very	bauld-gizzed	bold-faced
aathing	everything	bawbee	six pennies Scots
aa yer lane	alone	to be for	approve of
abeen	above	begack	unexpected surprise
Aest	the East	sic a begack	such a shock of
aet	eat		surprise
affa	very	begoud	began
aft	often	begunked	cheated, deceived
agee	off the straight	bejant	first year student at a
ain	own		Scottish University
aince mair	once more		(now St Andrews only),
air	early		from French, bejaune,
amang	among		bec jaune, a young bird,
ambry	cupboard		inexperienced youth
ampin	in a state of anxiety	belly-baum	comfort for the belly
ana	as well	ben	through the house; in
ance	once		the bedroom
ane	one	bere	type of barley grown in
ane tae anither	to one another		north of Scotland; four
anent	concerning		or six-row barley,
anidder	another		hardier, stronger than
anidder gaet	another way		ordinary two-row
apo, apu	upon		barley
Asaland	Asia	bere cake	barley scone
ase, asse	ashes	bield, bieldit	shelter; sheltered
aside	beside	biggin'	building
at	that	birks	birch trees
athin	inside, into	birsled	well cooked, with skin
ati	within		crackled
aucht	eight	birss	anger; angry winds
auld	old	bi smaa's	little by little
ava	at all	a bit o' a lee	a little shelter
awauk	awake	a bittie	for a short time
awfee (awful)	very	blae	blue
aye	always	blate	modest
ax	ask	bleezes	blazes
		bodach	old man
		bodle	two pennies Scots
baby clouts	baby clothes	brankie	badly behaved
baith	both	braw	splendid
barming	frothing of fermenting	bree	pour
	ale	breirin	germination

briggy stanes	footpath of flat stones laid in front of a house	*cowps*	overturns
brocht	brought	*crack*	talk, chat
brock	rubbish, food and vegetable scraps, leftovers	*cracken crouse*	chatting merrily or confidently
		cranreuch	hoar frost
brod	board	*cried*	called
brose	oatmeal to make a meal	*croodit roon*	crowded round
		cuist them throu her mind	pondered over them; turned them over in her mind
brü	broth		
brukken	broken		
brunt	burned	*curler – you for the curler!*	expression praising the curler's prowess
bubbly-jock	turkey		
budder	bother	*curran bun*	currant bun
never let bug	don't breathe a word		
busslins an redd	puddings and haggis		
by-ordinar	extraordinary	*da, de*	the
		daar	dare
		daated	indulged
		dan	then
caa'd	turned	*daud, dawd*	lump, large piece
caald	cold	*dauner*	stroll
callant	boy	*daurna*	daren't
canty	merry	*daursay*	daresay
caul	cold	*daw*	dawn
cauldrif(e)	intensely cold	*dee*	to you; do
caunels	candles	*deed ay*	indeed yes
champin	champing	*deeve*	annoy
chap	knock, strike, mash	*deil a haet*	not a whit
cheep	whisper	*dell*	delve
chiel	man	*dem*	them
chittered	shivered	*denty*	dainty
cholds	boys who had twelve months to complete in Heriot's Hospital	*der, dir*	there (is)
		dere, dey	there
		dey	they
chuckie-stanes	pebbles	*dicht*	wipe
clachan	village	*ding*	function
claes	clothes	*dirds*	knocks
cled	clothed	*dirl*	tingle
cleuch o' a craig	cleft in a rock; ravine in a crag	*dis*	does
		disjaskit an deen	downcast, exhausted
clooks	claws	*div*	do
clootie dumplin	dumpling boiled in a cloth	*dizzens*	dozens
		Dod	interjection, euphemism for 'God!'
clootie rug	rag rug		
Co	Co-operative store	*doddy mitten*	a worsted glove with division for thumb only
coggie	wooden drinking cup		
connie	corner	*doos*	doves
coorie doon	snuggle down	*dose*	small loaf of bread
corse	cross	*doot*	doubt

'doubles'	pupils dismissed at 1 pm instead of 12.30 and go home for the day. A double attendance is marked in the register
dour	stubborn
dowf	weary
dowie	dismal
dreich	miserable
dunch	push away
dunt	thump
dwined	withered
dy	your
dyke	drystone wall
een, e'en	eyes
eident	diligent
eyn	end
emmer	ember
fa	befall
fa?	who?
faan, fin	when
faain	falling
fa to thinkin	start to think
faased up	flattered
fae, frae	from
fail fauld-dyke	wall topped with turf, round a fold
faim	ale keg with froth of foam on it
fain	glad, content
fairly	completely
fan	small loaf of bread with crust on top, bottom and sides
fan (verb)	found
far, faur	where
farrer	farther
fash	trouble
feart	afraid
fecklessness	weakness, incompetence
fegs	emphatic expression, expressing surprise
ferlie	marvel
fey	portentious

fike	worry
fin oot	find out
fite	white
flachterin	fluttering
fleein	flying
fleer	floor
fleein	flying
fleggit	frightened
fleyed	scared
flicht	flight
flist ower	hurry or fly over
florin	a two shilling piece
flyte	scold
foo	how
forbye, furbye	as well
forenent	in front of
forgie	forgive
fortaivert	ragged, tattered
fremmyt	unfamiliar
frichtsome	frightening
frichtit	frightened
frien	friend
frit	fruit
fuffin lowe	smoking, hissing flames
fun, funn	found
fur a wee	for a short time
fut, fut's	what, what is
fyles	at times
fyou bit words	few short words
gadderie	gathering
gae, gaen	gave, given
gaed, geed	went
gaen, gaun	going
gane	gone
gangerels	tramps
gang, geng	go
gang wantin	go without
garred	caused
gars him grue	makes him shudder with fear or disgust
gate	way
gat weel	became well
a get sicht	a great deal
gey	very
gie, gie's	give, give us
gilravaged	in state of confusion

gilt	metaphorical; a young sow		*happin*	covering; hopping
gin	in readiness for		*hard*	heard
girnel	meal chest		*haudin doun*	restraining
gloaming-fa	dusk		*hauf-croun*	half-a-crown, two shillings and sixpence, old money
gled	kite (bird); buzzard			
glintit	shone		*haun*	hand
glore	glory		*haverin*	talking nonsense
glow'ring	staring		*heck*	rack for fodder in a stable, manger
göd furt	went forth			
Govies	governors		*heelster-gowdie*	head over heels
gowdspink	goldfinch		*heicher*	higher
grane	groan		*heicht*	height
grat	wept		*hender-en*	in the end
gravat	scarf		*G.H.H.*	George Heriot's Hospital, built 1628-59, bequeathed by George Heriot; now George Heriot's School.
gree	agree			
greetin'	weeping			
grete	great			
grice	pig			
grumphie	pig		*hertstane or sten*	hearthstone
gruppit	gripped		*het pint*	hot spiced ale drunk at Hogmanay
gryte	great			
guid	good		*hinmaist*	final
guid-sister	sister-in-law		*hird*	care for
guizards	guisers		*hirsel'*	herself
gulsa	jaundice		*hissel*	himself
gurly	angry		*hit*	it
gyang	going		*hoops*	hopes
			horn	prow
			hotterin	boiling
Auld Haa	Old Hall House – formerly a laird's house		*howdumdeid*	dead of night
			howes	hollows
haar	cold mist or fog		*howff*	inn
had	hold		*howkin*	digging
hae, haena	have, have not, don't have		*huemin*	dusk, evening twilight
			hurley bed	truckle bed
haem	home		*hushie baloo*	hushaby
haill	whole			
hailie shooers	hail showers		*ida, idda*	in the
hain	stint		*ile*	(castor) oil
hairst	harvest		*ilka*	every
hairst mön	harvest moon		*ilkane*	each one
hale an feer	complete, indomitable		*ill-trickit*	evil
hale be	good health to		*ir*	are
halflins	teenagers		*in-by, inby*	inside, close beside
hameower	simple		*is*	has
handsel	gift or money given on the first Monday of the New Year			

jalouse	suspect
jaud	jade, perverse woman
jeuk	play
jooglie	wobbly, shaky
Jorsaland	Palestine
joukie-daidles	playful fondling
jucks	ducks
keek	peep
keekit	glanced
kenna	don't know
kent, weel-kent	known, well known
keep dir herts	keep up, or cheer their hearts
kin	kind
kinda faert	rather afraid
kirn	butter churn
knabbie	person of rank
knaps	general name for schoolboys
knowes	hollows
kyent, kyentna	knew, did not know
kyuntrie	country
latchy	lagging
laan, laun	land
laich	low
laek	like
laer	learning
Lammas Fair	a traditional market held in Kirkwall, 2nd Tuesday of August
lane, her	on her own
lanesome	lonely
lauch	laugh
lawd	senior boy's title during his last six months in school
leuk	look
lib	pounds
lichtsome	cheerful, carefree
licks	thrashing
lift	sky
liggin	lying
lillilu	lullaby
liltin	singing
link'd	ran briskly
lintie	linnet
lippenin	expecting

littlins	children
lochan	small loch
loe	love
a lok mair	a good quantity, a great deal more
loof	palm of the hand
loon	boy, laddie
loot	let
loup	jump, leap
lowed	shone
lug	ear
three-lugged cog	wooden drinking vessel, three handles
luk	look
lum	chimney, lum hat – top hat
luntan	smoking
maist	most
mait	meat
Mammie	matron of George Heriot's Hospital
masel	myself
maun	must
med	made
midder	mother
min', mind	remember
mineer	uproar, fuss; debris
minnie	grandmother
mirk	dusk
mirl	mix
moolins	crumbs
moorie-blind	blinding blizzard
morn's nicht	tomorrow night
mous	mouths
muckle	great
mutchkin	$1/4$ pt Scots, ($3/4$ pt imp); a container of this capacity
nab	grab
nabbit	struck
nae mair	no more
nappy	ale
narra	narrow
nebs	noses
nedder	neither
neebors	neighbours
neen	none

neeps	turnips	*quate*	quiet
Ne'erday	New Year's Day	*quernstone*	grinding stone, mill-stone
neive	fist		
nock	clock	*queyo*	calf female calf
nor	than	*quine*	lass
nowt	cattle		
nyakit	naked		
		raep	line or rail, stretched between two fixed points for hanging things out to dry
oagit	crawled		
onywey	anyway		
örie boddie	unusual person, suggesting supernatural	*raised laek*	highly strung, with a peculiar aura
orra cloot	odd rag	*rale*	really, very
		rantan	making merry
		ream	foam
peck	2 galls, dry measure	*redding-up*	tidying up
peely-wally	pallid, ill-looking	*reeks*	smokes, steams
peenies	pinafores	*reestin*	roosting
peerie	little	*restin paets*	peats used to bank up a fire overnight
Peerie Sea	land-locked water, bordered by shoreline at eastern end of Kirkwall and the main highway to the West Mainland, once fully tidal	*roch*	rough
		rottans	rats
		rowed up, rowit	wrapped up
		ruch	rough
		ruifs	roofs
		ruisin	extolling
peerie tings	little ones, children		
pig	stone hot-water bottle	*sailland*	sailing
pin	latch	*sair*	sorely
pint o the sma	pint of small beer	*sanct*	saint
pit furrit	put forward	*sanna*	shall not
pitten	putting	*saps*	small pieces of bread, soaked or boiled in milk
playocks	toys, playthings		
plooin	ploughing		
pock	poke, bag		
pooch	pocket	*sark*	shirt
pookit	pecked	*sassinger*	sausage
Poussie Baudrons	traditional nickname for a cat	*say*	news
		saxt	sixth
pouthers	powders	*scalin*	spilling
pow	head	*schule*	school
priggin sair	pleading anxiously	*scraunin*	scrounging
puckle	small quantity	*screich o day*	dawn
pu'd	pulled	*screw-top*	glass beer bottle, with stone-ware top
puir	poor		
in a pule	steaming	*scrimpit*	frugal, scanty
pun	pound	*scruntit*	scraggy
pund	enclosure for sheep	*scud*	smack

scunner	disgust
scurt	bosom
seik	sick
Serkland	Africa
shair	sure
sheeld	child
shin, shinner	soon, sooner
shivs	shoves
shön	soon
shön, shoon	shoes
shörely	surely
shour	shower
shuggar	sugar
shuir	sure
sib	related
sic a	such a
sicht	sight
siller	money
sin	since
skelp	slap, strike
skleuterin	floundering
skirie-like	dressed in gaudy clothes
skites	slides across plate
skyin	skin
slee	sly
sklentit	glanced
smeddum	spirit
smore	covering of snow
smoor	cover thickly
snaa	snow
snashters	contemptuous tone in speaking of sweets, cakes or trashy food
sneck	latch
sneeshum	snuff
snell	bitter
snod	snug
someen	someone
sonsie	fat
sood	should
soon	sound
soop	sweep her up
soopit	swept
sotter	chaos
Souter	native of Selkirk
spak	spoke
speired, speirin	asked, asking
speldert	split, pulled apart
speug	sparrow
staavin	dashing, purposeful
stanein	standing
steer	stir
steir and stour	stir and dust
stieres-man	helmsman
stirkie	young bullock
stishie	uproar
stöd	stood
stot	young, castrated bullock
stoup	tankard
stourin	hurrying
stovies	potatoes cooked with dripping, onions, sometimes small pieces of meat
strae	straw
strawing	strewing
stüde, stuid	stood, hung
suid	should
Sundee	Sunday
sune, suner	soon, sooner
some at sune ta be	some that will soon be born
swack	moist, juicy
swats	weak beer, newly brewed
swealed	wrapped
swear, sweirt	unwilling
sweein	stinging
swink	splash
swither	hesitate
syke	a marshy hollow
syne	thereupon, since
ta	to
taen	taken
tairge	target
tak tent	pay attention
tangies	tangerine oranges
tattie, tawtie	potato
tauld, telt	told
tell	tale
thae	those
thair	there
thegither	together
thocht, tocht	thought

thole	bear, endure
thowe	thaw
toom	empty
thrang	crowded
thraw	wring
throwe, trow	through
til	to, unto
til ither	to one another
tink	think
tinkler	tinker; travelling person who works in metal
Tod Lowrie	nickname for a fox
toty	tiny
tout-soup	potato soup
touzie	ruffled, dishevelled
tree, threed	three, third
troch	cattle trough
trowe, trowie	troll
tryst (noun)	assignation; (verb) to meet
trystit	betrothed
tü	too
tu	you
twal	twelve
ün	warmth
uncan, unco	strange
this unco	this strange thing
unco thrang	great throng
uncolie frichtit	very much afraid
vaige	journey
vaigin the causey	wandering along the street
voar	spring
vratch	wretch
waakened	wakened
waakrife	wakeful
wadder	weather
wae, waesome	sorrow, sorrowful
wale oot	choose, select
war	were
Wark	school building
warl	world

wasna	wasn't
wasterfu	extravagant
waur	were
weans	children
wearit	wearied
weird	mysterious knowledge
weird to dree	a fate to endure
werenae	weren't
whaar, whaur	where
what they could	as fast as they could drive
whatn	what kind of
whause	whose
wheen	a small number
wheepled	whistled
whilk	which
whin	when
whit fur no?	why not?
whit wey?	why?
wi', wie	with
wid	would
wids	woods
wiks	weeks
win	find his way
windaesole	window sill
windros	wondrous
winkie-wee	tiny
winna	won't
wirld	world
wirna	wasn't
wirsels	ourselves
wis	us
wisht	be quiet
wiss	wish
wonn'd	dwelt
wordy	worthy
wort	brewing
wran	wren
wuldna	would not, wouldn't
wunner	wonder
wur	our
wye	way
yaised	used
yer	your
ye'se	you shall
ye s'ken	you will know
yestreen	yesterday

yett	door	*yowes*	ewes
yill	ale	*yowled*	wailed
yin, yins	one, ones	*yowt*	cry
yird	earth	*yun*	yon, that one over there
yon byre	that byre over there		

G A E L I C

mo, m'	my	*mhaccan*	little son
ghaol	darling, beloved	*a`lainn*	beautiful
ghra'dh	love	*ceutach*	beloved
is	and	*chan fhiu mi-fheinn*	I am not worthy
eudal thu	dearest one	*bhith'd dhàil*	(to be) in your presence
iunntas	wealth		
ùr	new		
eibhneas	delight		

A C K N O W L E D G E M E N T S

Poetry, Prose and Recipes – Owners of Copyright and Sources

AUTHOR	TITLE	SOURCE
–	An Latha-Feill Muire	*Tiomnadh Nuadh* (New Testament), The National Bible Society of Scotland, 1935.
Annand, J K	Jennie Wren; Robin Reidbreist Santa; Snawman Jack Frost (1, 2); On Hogmanay	*Sing it aince for Pleisure,* Macdonald, 1965. *Twice with Joy,* Macdonald, 1973. *Thrice to Show Ye,* Macdonald, 1979.
Anon (*or not attributed*)	A Riddle; A Spice Cup for Macgregor; Riddle; The Robins; Welcome Little Robin	– – –
Athole, His Grace the Duke of	Athole Brose	*Fan Fare,* Pitlochry Festival Theatre, 1978.
Baillie, Jamieson	Off for the Holidays; Heigh-ho, for Winter Days …	*Reminiscences of George Heriot's Hospital,* E & S Livingstone.
Ballantine, James	Castles in the Air	*The Scottish Orpheus,* Paterson & Sons, 1897.
Barclay, William	Matthew's Version of the Story of the Good News Prayer for Christmas Night	*The New Testament: a translation by William Barclay,* published by Arthur James Ltd, One Cranbourne Road, London. *The Plain Man's Book of Prayers,* Fontana, 1959.
Baxter, Ena	Macduff Christmas Cake	*Ena Baxter's Scottish Cook Book,* Johnston and Bacon, 1974.
Bejant, Augustus	Invocation to Black Bun	The *Glasgow University Magazine.*
Bell, J J	An Invitation; New Year's Eve	*Wee MacGreegor,* Grafton Books, 1977.
Blackhall, Sheena	Christmas Blues Hen's Lament Year's End	*Fite Doo/Black Crow,* Keith Murray Publications, 1989. *The Cyard's Kist,* Rainbow Enterprises, 1984. *Hame-Drauchtit,* Rainbow Enterprises, 1987.
Bowie, Janetta	Candle Culprits	*Penny Buff,* Constable, 1975.

Acknowledgements

Brown, George Mackay	The Midwinter Music – Christmas *and* New Year	*An Orkney Tapestry*, Victor Gollancz, 1969.
Burns, Robert	The Twa Dogs	*Poems, Chiefly in the Scottish Dialect* – The Kilmarnock Edition, 1786.
	The Marriage of Robin Redbreast and the Wren (*attributed*)	
Chambers, Robert	Robinets and Jenny Wrens … ; The Marriage of Robin Redbreast and the Wren; Please tae help the Guizards …	*Popular Rhymes of Scotland*, Chambers, 1826.
Cocker, W D	The Auld Year; Hogmanay; The Bubbly-Jock; The Roarin' Game	*Poems Scots and English*, Brown, Son & Ferguson, 1932.
Craig, Elizabeth (*recipes*)	Bacon and Mushroom Rolls; Boston Cream; Brown Gravy; Chestnut and Oyster Stuffing; Cranberry Sauce; Hogmanay Fare; Roastit Bubbly-Jock; Sausagemeat Stuffing; Stone Cream	*The Scottish Cookery Book*, Andre Deutsch, 1956.
Cruickshank, Helen B	Background	*Ten Northeast Poets*, Aberdeen University 1985.
Daiches, David	December Dusk in the South Side	*Two Worlds*, Sussex University Press, 1957.
Dods, Meg (*recipe*)	Het Pint	*The Scots Cellar*, Granada Publishing, 1981.
Drew, Mrs T S	Mince Pies	*Fan Fare*, Pitlochry Festival Theatre, 1978.
Duncan, Jane	The New Year Himself	*My friends the Misses Kindness*, Macmillan, 1974.
Edinburgh College of Domestic Science	Brussels Sprouts au Jus	*The Edinburgh Book of Advanced Cookery Recipes*, Thomas Nelson and Son, 1933.
	Apple Sauce; Boiled Carrots	*The Edinburgh Book of Plain Cookery Recipes*, Thomas Nelson and Son, 1932.
Elliot, Walter	The Christmas Tree 1976	*The Clash-ma-Clavers Chapbook*, 1984.
Fraser, Amy Stewart	Child in the Manger	*Roses in December*, Routledge.

Fraser, Amy Stewart (*cont'd*)	A Boxing Day to Remember; Christmas at the Manse of Crathie; The Last Night of the Year; Yule's come and Yule's gane	*Hills of Home*, Routledge, 1973.
Glasgow and West of Scotland College of Domestic Science	Baked Ham	The Glasgow Cookery Book, 1962, John Smith and Son (Glasgow) Ltd and Glasgow Caledonian University.
Glennie, Evelyn	Stovies for Hogmanay	*Good Vibrations,* Hutchinson, 1990.
Gray, Alexander	Christmas Carol	*Any Man's Life,* Blackwell, 1924.
Greig, Marjory	Handsel Monday 1926; Thoughts for Yule 1989	Unpublished.
Greig, Marjory (*Traditional; owerset by*)	Awa in a Manger (*words*); Christmas comes; The Christmas Guizards (*words*); Christmas is comin; Cock Robin's Courtship; God be Here; Hey for Sunday; The Nor Wind; On Christmas Eve; Plum Duff; A Riddle; Robinets and Jenny Wrens … ; The Robins; Ungratefu Jenny	– – – – – – – –
Guild, Prue	Carol for the Handicapped	*Just an Idea*, 1986.
Henry, Claire	Da Trow's Christmas	*Shetland Life*, 1985.
Horne, David	The Ba'	*Songs of Orkney, The Orkney Herald,* 1923.
Inglis, John	Victorian Edinburgh Diary – Christmas and 1880 comes in	*A Victorian Edinburgh Diary,* Ramsay Head Press, 1984.
Ireland, Kenneth	Claret Cup	*Fan Fare,* Pitlochry Festival Theatre, 1978.
Jamieson, John	Handsel Monday	*Dictionary of the Scottish Language,* 1818.
Jay	Christmas	*New Shetlander,* 1985.
Kirk, Mrs E W (*recipes*)	Red Cabbage to Pickle; Savoury Potatoes; Clear Soup; Casserole of Potatoes; Moonshine; A Christmas Dish for the Bairns	*Tried Favourites,* J B Fairgrieve, 1919.

$$\overbrace{\qquad\qquad}\ \left(\ Acknowledgements\ \right)\ \overbrace{\qquad\qquad}$$

Lindsay, Maurice	Hogmanay 1963	*One Later Day,* Brookside Press, 1964.
Lockhart, John Gibson	Hogmanay at Abbotsford	*Life of Scott*, 1837.
Macdonald, Mary	Santa Claus was no Big Deal	Unpublished, 1994.
McLintock, Mrs *(recipes)*	For a Goose-Pye To make Short Bread	*Receipts for Cookery & Pastrywork 1736,* Aberdeen University Press, 1986.
McNeill, F Marian	Feather Fowlie; An Ormidale Steak Pie … ; Black Bun *(recipe)* Het Pint Scots Currant Loaf; Black Bun *(verse)*	*Recipes from Scotland,* Albyn Press, 1946. *The Scots Cellar,* Granada Publishing, 1981. *The Scots Kitchen,* Blackie & Son, 1929.
Marwick, Ernest	Kirkwall to the Ba'	*The Folklore of Orkney and Shetland,* Batsford.
Miller, Christian	The Castle Celebrates	*A Childhood in Scotland,* John Murray, 1981.
Morrice, Ken	The Bairnie Jesus – A Carol	*The Living Doric,* Charles Murray Memorial Trust, 1985.
Muir, Christine	Island Advent; Island Yule	*Orkney Days,* Scotsman Publications, 1986.
Murison, David	January – Ne'erday Handsel Monday	*The Scottish Year,* Mercat Press, 1982. *First Statistical Account* I, 1791-98.
Murray, Charles	Winter	*Hamewith,* Aberdeen University Press, 1982.
Ogston, David	Carol Service	*White Stone Country,* Ramsay Head Press, 1986.
Penny, George	New Year's Day in Perth; Handsel Monday	*Traditions of Perth,* William Culross & Son, 1986.
Picken, E	31st December – Hogmanay	*Dictionary of the Scottish Language,* 1818.
Ramsay, Allan	*From* Elegy on Lucky Woods	Thomas Ruddiman, 1718.
Rich, Lilianne Grant	A Christmas Prayer Nativity	*The Horn Speen,* Rainbow Enterprises, 1983. *Echo of Many Voices*, AUP, 1980.

Acknowledgements

Scott, Sir Walter	'The Scottish Labourer ... '	*Life of Scott*, 1837, John Gibson Lockhart.
Scottish Women's Rural Institutes	Granny's Plum Pudding with Caudle Sauce; Trifle; Syllabub	*Traditional Scottish Recipes*, Scottish Women's Rural Institutes.
Smith, Jamie A	Nae Room; Nae Brankie Bairn; Christmas Contrast; Efter Hogmanay	*Poems o Scotland*, 1986.
Soutar, William	Open the Door	*The Poems of William Soutar*, Scottish Academic Press, 1988; courtesy of the National Library of Scotland.
Stevenson, Robert Louis	New Year's Weather	*Edinburgh, 1879*, Seeley & Co Ltd.
Stuart, Jamie	The Foretellin o Jesus; The Birth o Jesus; The Angel's Sang; The Bairn is Named	*A Scots Gospel*, Saint Andrew Press, 1985, 1992 (*revised*).
Sutherland, D G	Letter to my Grandchildren	*Letters to my Grandchildren*, 1986.
Sutherland, Stella	Second Christmas	*Shetland Life*, 1984; *A celebration and other poems*, 1991.
	New Year comes in	*Shetland Life*, 1991.
Traditional	Ther cam a Ship	Reproduced from *Musica Britannica*, Vol XV (edited by Helena Shire); by kind permission of Stainer & Bell Ltd, 1964.
Traditional (*misc*)	Christmas comes but ance a Year; Christmas is comin; Cock Robin's Courtship; Cry Yule; God be Here; Hey for Sunday; On Christmas Eve; The Nor Wind; Plum Duff; Yule's come and Yule's gane	– – – – – – –
Vagaland	Nativity Play; Christmas Bells; The Star; Da Tree Kings	*The Collected Poems of Vagaland*, Shetland Times Ltd, 1978.
Weir, Molly	Grannie's New Year; Redding-up for the New Year; Yule's come and Yule's gane	*Shoes were for Sunday*, Grafton Books, 1970.

Acknowledgements

Williamson, Duncan	The Dog and the Manger; Tatties from Chuckie-stanes	*Tell me a story for Christmas*, Canongate, 1987.
Williamson, Clement J	Old Christmas in Shetland	1991.
Wilson, Marjorie	New Boots for Santa; The Third Santa; Lamplight, Moonlight and the Glint of Ice; 'Over sixty years ago … '	*The Scotsman*, 1969.
–	The Forgotten Children of Bethlehem	*The Sunday Post*, 1991.
–	26th December – Sweetie Scone Day	*Gentlemen's Magazine*, July 1790.
–	29th December – The Tay Bridge Disaster, 1879	*Dundee Courier and Argus*, 29th December, 1879.

ACKNOWLEDGEMENTS
Music and Words to Music – Owners of Copyright and Sources

TITLE	COMPOSER/WRITER	SOURCE
Auld Year, The	Sinclair, Margaret (*music*)	–
Awa in a Manger	Chrodh Chailein (*tune*) Traditional Gaelic Air J Kirkpatrick (*words*) *owerset by* Marjory Greig	*Children Praising*, Oxford University Press, 1937.
Child in the Manger	Bunessan (*tune*) Traditional Gaelic Air Mairi MacDonald (*words*) Lachlan MacBean (*trans*)	*Church Hymnary* III, Oxford University Press, 1973.
Christmas Guizards, The (The Gloucestershire Wassail)	R Vaughan Williams (*collected*) Traditional (*words*) *owerset by* Marjory Greig	Trans. used with this setting from *Ted Heath Carols*, 1977, by permission of Oxford University Press.
Christmas Tree March, The	Angus Cameron (*music*)	*David Glen's collection of Highland Bag-pipe Music*, David Glen, 1897.
Hogmanay Song	Margaret Sinclair (*music*) Traditional (*words*)	–
Mary's Sang ('Hushie Baloo')	Maureen McDougal (*music*) Joyce Collie (*words*)	*Life and Work*, 1984.
New Christmas	John Anderson (*music*)	*A Selection of the most approved Highland Strathspeys, etc* 1791.
New Year's Day	James Stewart Robertson (*music*)	*Davie's Caledonian Repository*, Wood & Co, 1829.
Sunty	Traditional (*music*) Adam Hamilton (*arrang.*) James D Glennie (*words*)	Rainbow Enterprises and *The Living Doric*, Charles Murray Memorial Trust, 1985.
Taladh Chriosta ('Christ Child's Lullaby')	Traditional Gaelic Air Isle of Eriskay	–

Acknowledgements

We are aa Queen Mary's   Traditional (*music/words*)   *The Greig-Duncan Folk Song Collection,*
 Men   Aberdeen University Press, 1987.

Yule's come and   Traditional (*music*)   *Fifty Traditional Scottish Nursery Rhymes,*
 Yule's gane   Alfred Moffat (*arrang.*)   1933.

THE CONTRIBUTORS

Birthplaces and Dates

Annand, J K	Edinburgh	1908-1993
Baillie, Jamieson	Edinburgh	*circa* 1860
Ballantine, James	Edinburgh	1808-1877
Barclay, William	Wick, Caithness	1907-1978
Bell, J J	Glasgow	1871-1934
Blackhall, Sheena	Aberdeen	1947-
Bowie, Janetta	Greenock, Renfrewshire	1907-
Brown, George Mackay	Stromness, Orkney	1921-
Burns, Robert	Alloway, Ayrshire	1759-1796
Chambers, Robert	Peebles	1802-1871
Cocker, W D	Glasgow	1882-1970
Collie, Joyce	Aberdeen	1929-
Cruikshank, Helen B	Hillside, Angus	1886-1975
Daiches, David	Sunderland	1912-
Duncan, Jane	Glasgow	1910-1976
Elliot, Walter	Selkirk	1934-
Fraser, Amy Stewart	Manse of Glen Gairn	
	Aberdeenshire	1892-1985
Glennie, Evelyn	Aberdeen	1965-
Glennie, James D	Udney, Aberdeenshire	1930-
Gray, Alexander	Dundee	1882-1968
Greig, Marjory	Edinburgh	1917-
Guild, Prue	Southsea, Hants	1917-
Henry, Claire	Lerwick, Shetland	1974-
Horne, David	Kirkwall, Orkney	1876-1940
Inglis, John	Edinburgh	1850-1892
Jay (Janet Hughson Smith)	Stoer Head Lighthouse, Sutherland	1926-
Lindsay, Maurice	Glasgow	1918-
Lockhart, John Gibson	Cambusnethan, Lanarkshire	1794-1854
MacBean, Lachlan	Kiltarlity, Inverness-shire	1853-1931
MacDonald, Mairi	Ardtun, Isle of Mull	1817-1890
MacDonald, Mary	Morar, Inverness-shire	1929-
McDougal, Maureen	Aberdeen	1935-
McNeill, F Marian	St Mary's Holm, Orkney	1885-1973
Marwick, Ernest	Fursan, Evie, Orkney	1915-1977
Miller, Christian	The House of Monymusk,	
	Aberdeenshire	1920-
Muir, Christine	Leith	1939-

Murison, David	Fraserburgh	1913-
Murray, Charles	Alford, Aberdeenshire	1864-1941
Ogston, David	Ellon, Aberdeenshire	1945-
Penny, George	Perth	1771-1850
Ramsay, Allan	Leadhills, Lanarkshire	1684-1758
Rich, Lilianne Grant	Glenlivet, Aberdeenshire	1909-
Scott, Sir Walter	Edinburgh	1771-1832
Sinclair, Margaret	Vancouver, Canada	1915-
Smith, Jamie A	Innerpeffray, Perthshire	1910-
Stevenson, Robert Louis	Edinburgh	1850-1894
Stuart, Jamie	Glasgow	1920-
Sutherland, D G	Cuppaster, South Yell, Shetland	1914-1989
Vagaland (E A Robertson)	Walls, Shetland	1909-1973
Weir, Molly	Glasgow	1920-
Williams, Ralph Vaughan	Down Ampney, Gloucestershire	1982-1958
Williamson, Clement J	Scalloway, Shetland	1904-1994
Williamson, Duncan	In a traveller bow tent on the shores of Loch Fyne, Argyll	1928-
Wilson, Marjorie	Edinburgh	1911-